D1258772

THE BOOK OF

COFFEE

A GOURMET'S GUIDE

Francesco and
Riccardo Illy

ABBEVILLE PRESS ■ PUBLISHERS
New York ■ London ■ Paris

LAYOUT: Marc Walter
GRAPHIC COORDINATION: Simona Aguzzoni
TRANSLATION: Pamela Swinglehurst

PHOTOGRAPHS: Francesco Illy

SOURCES OF ILLUSTRATIONS:
Lauros-Giraudon Agency, Paris
Roger-Viollet Agency, Paris
Arbook Archive, Paris
Illycaffè Archive, Trieste
Enrico Castruccio, Milan
Jacobs Suchards Museum, Zurich
SIPA Editions, Paris
Tropen Museum, Amsterdam

Published by arrangement with Arnoldo
Mondadori Editore S.p.A., Milano

Copyright © 1989 Arnoldo Mondadori Editore
S.p.A., Milano. Translation copyright © 1992
Arnoldo Mondadori Editore S.p.A., Milano. All
rights reserved under international copyright con-
ventions. No part of this work may be reproduced
or utilized, in any form or by any means, electronic or mechanical, including photocopying, record-
ing, or by any information storage and retrieval
system, without permission in writing from the
publisher. Inquiries should be directed to
Abbeville Press, 488 Madison Avenue, New York,
NY 10022. Printed and bound in Italy.

First American edition

Library of Congress Cataloging-in-Publication
Data

Illy, Francesco.
      The book of coffee: a gourmet's guide /
Francesco and Riccardo Illy ; [translation,
Pamela Swinglehurst ; photographs, Francesco
Illy]. — 1st American ed.
            p.   cm.
      Translated from the Italian.
      Includes bibliographical references.
      ISBN 1-55859-321-7
      1. Coffee. I. Illy, Riccardo. II. Title.
TX415.I44   1992
641.3'373—dc20   91-33431
                                             CIP

Why another book on coffee? A number of such books have been written – and I've read and commented on just about all of them – but the way I see it, the ones by coffee experts have been too polarized or sectorial, while those written by people not connected with the coffee business have been vague and approximate. This book, on the other hand, is different because it's on a specific subject: the evolution of coffee, from bean to espresso.

The espresso method of making coffee is the king of all coffee-making methods because the greatest amount of "noble" substances are extracted; that is, those which give the coffee drink its body, aroma and flavour. Consistently high quality levels, however, are not easy to achieve and require having a thorough knowledge of all phases of the subject, from the plant to the harvesting, to the type of processing required according to the country of origin, and so on. The Illy family's traditional love for coffee has been like a veritable "disease" that has spread through three generations. Having been weaned on tiny spoonfuls of espresso coffee, the authors were able to cultivate a very early appreciation for this exceptional beverage, which matured into the profound love that inspired the writing and illustrating of this book. Through close cooperation, they achieved their goal of making this complex subject very clear, easy to understand, and up-to-date, both as regards Italy and other countries. This is particularly important today because of espresso coffee's widespread popularity which is extending to all corners of the globe. The priceless information contained in this book will not only be interesting for long-standing lovers of espresso coffee, but will also satisfy the curiosity of the newcomers to the everwidening circle of espresso coffee devotees. Moreover, in my opinion, this book also pays homage to those who have dedicated their lives to coffee and to those who love and appreciate a good cup of espresso.

Ernesto Illy

THE
NATURE
OF
COFFEE

The coffee plant is a shrub that belongs to the family Rubiaceae, genus *Coffea*. Some dozens of species of the genus *Coffea* are known, but only two are significant in economic terms: *Coffea arabica* and *Coffea canephora*, being the only two that are cultivated on a large scale. Each of these two species comprises several varieties, some derived from natural mutations and some the results of genetic engineering. After Prospero Alpino's brief description in *De Plantis Aegypti* (1592), we find the first botanical description of the coffee plant, called *Jasminum arabicanum*, by A. de Jussieu (1713). The present classification of the *Coffea* species dates back to the 1940's and is due chiefly to the work of Chevalier and Lebrun.

The plant consists of one or more trunks from which stem the primary branches which in turn divide into secondary branches: only the latter, if damaged, will regrow. In its wild state the plant grows to a height of 8-10 metres whereas in plantations, to facilitate care and cropping, the plants are kept to a height of 2-2.5 metres. The leaves grow in opposite pairs, are 10-15 centimetres long and oval or lanceolate in shape. They are deep rich green in colour, glossy and fleshy on their upper surface, and overall are not unlike laurel leaves, with the characteristic wavy edge. The flowers are white and always grow in clusters of two or three together, reaching almost 2 centimetres in size. The flowering season is very brief, only a few days, but during this period the flowers emit a very strong pleasant perfume, and provide a real feast for the insects that visit them for their nectar. Pollination is only neces-

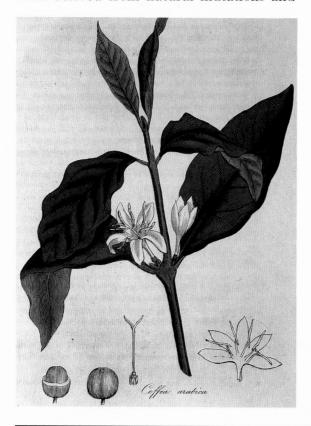

Coffea arabica

Facing title: A plant of *Coffea arabica* species with its branches laden with berries. *Above:* Tip of coffee-plant branch showing how leaves grow in pairs: the white, highly fragrant flowers grow where the leaves attach to the branches: as they ripen, the berries change colour from green to yellow and, finally, red. *Side:* One of the ripe berries shown is cut open to show the outer skin, pulp and beans. Two other beans are shown still wrapped in their thin, white gold-tinted membranes (parchment).

sary for the species *Coffea canephora* because the *arabica* is autogamous, that is to say its flowers can pollinate themselves. The fruit which develops from the ovary of the fertilized flower is called drupe or berry; it is about 15 millimetres in diameter and turns bright red when fully ripe. The outer covering of the drupe is a thick pulpy skin, the exocarp, which encloses a layer of jelly-like pulp, the mesocarp, about 2 millimetres thick. Inside this are the seeds or beans; these are enclosed in a thick, whitish-coloured protective endocarp, commonly called "parchment". Beneath the parchment, completely encasing each individual bean, is another fine skin called the "silver skin". There are generally two beans inside each berry; some-

Two native workers on a coffee plantation. The thick foliage of the tall trees protect the precious coffee plants. As can be seen, the plants are kept trimmed to a height of about 2.5 metres to facilitate both maintenance and harvesting.

times, through insufficient pollination, there is only a single round bean, called "peaberry" coffee; there are rarely three beans. The seeds or beans of the coffee berry are an elongated oval in shape, convex on one side and flat on the other, with a deep furrow.

They average about 10 millimetres in length, weigh about 0.15 grams each and are green in colour, tinged with shades varying from grey to blue or from red to brown. These beans are the only part of the fruits of the coffee plant that are used: the rest is discarded during processing.

Arabica and Robusta

The two species of coffee plant of economic significance are *Coffea arabica* and *Coffea canephora*, commonly referred to as Arabica and Robusta. The bulk of world production is from these species, with two other cultivated species, *Coffea liberica* and *Coffea excelsa*, playing a minor commercial role. Arabica is more widespread than Robusta, accounting for about three quarters of world production. Although the roasted beans of both these species are very similar, there are marked differences between the two plants and their seeds. Firstly, there are genetic differences: Arabica has 44 chromosomes whereas Robusta

has only half that number. The plants themselves, although similar, also differ slightly in the shape and colour of their leaves and flowers, and more particularly in the height they reach if they are not pruned: Arabica grows to 6-8 metres, Robusta to 8-10.

As the common name Robusta suggests,

this plant is markedly more resistant both to parasites and diseases and also to the heat: Robusta plants can withstand temperatures above 30 °C for several days whereas Arabica plants will suffer after only a few days. For both species, on the other hand, frost is fatal. The Arabica species is particularly sensitive to a disease called *Hemileia vastatrix*, which entirely destroyed the plantations in Ceylon that were subsequently converted to tea. Despite the use of modern pesticides,

Left: Antigua, Guatemala, where the coffee is grown on the slopes of "El Volcán", the extinct volcano seen in the background. The fog that frequently develops on the slopes during the night is evaporated by the early morning sun, which drops the temperature below freezing. It only takes a few minutes for the settling cold air to damage the leaves of young coffee plants. *Above:* The frozen leaves look like they have been burned.

the fight against this disease presents great difficulties, especially at lower altitudes; in fact it is only at altitudes over 900 metres above sea level that it can easily be defeated. This explains why the plantations of Arabica are found at altitudes of 900-2000 metres in zones practically never affected by frost whereas Robusta plantations are generally situated at altitudes of 200-300 metres in markedly hotter and more humid areas. Considering the greater costs entailed in cultivating plants at high altitude, often on steeply sloping ground, in addition to the greater quantity of pesticides and the greater amount of care required by the Arabica species, it is not surprising that the beans harvested from these plants have a higher market value, reflecting their superior quality.

But the most obvious differences are found in the seed or bean itself: the Arabica bean is flatter, more elongated, and the furrow on its flat surface is curved; it is a fairly deep green in colour, sometimes with a bluish tinge. The Robusta bean on the other hand is more convex and roundish in shape, the furrow is almost straight and it is normally a pale green in colour with brownish or greyish tinges. Even after roasting, if you look at them carefully you can see the difference in shape of the beans of the two species. From the chemical viewpoint the greatest disparity is in the percentage of caffeine contained in the beans: 1-1.7 per cent in Arabica and 2-4.5 per cent in Robusta. Robusta beans also contain a greater quantity of chlorogenic acids, substances that can upset the digestion if they exceed a certain level. The two species are also different "in the cup": Arabica is milder and more aromatic, distinctly less sharp and bitter.

A berry falls to the ground and embarks on a new adventure

There are two main ways in which a new coffee plant is grown: from seed or from cuttings. The former is the more common method, and makes it possible to cross different varieties with a view to improving the characteristics of the plant; the second method on the other hand ensures perfect

Above: An overall view of a nursery. The sprouts – so-called "little soldiers" – are later transplanted and take from 3 to 4 years to yield their first harvest. *Side:* The two most common types of beans are the *Coffea canephora* and the *Coffea arabica*. The former is rounder, with a straight cleft down its middle, while the latter is more oblong and has a curving cleft down its middle. *Right:* "Little soldiers" in their bed of fine, richly-organic nursery soil.

replication of the mother-plant, avoiding unwanted mutations.

When propagating from seed, the greatest attention is paid to the harvesting of the berries, which must be perfectly ripe, and to the selection of the seeds themselves. This operation, carried out entirely by hand, consists of choosing the reddest and most regular berries and carefully pressing them with the fingers to squeeze out the two seeds in their parchment covering, without damaging them.

The seeds are then immersed in water: those that float to the surface are discarded, as are those of imperfect colour. Those seeds which have passed the test are finally placed 1-3 centimetres apart on a bed of selected soil rich in humus, in suitable wooden frames, and covered with another thin layer of soil.

This is then liberally watered and lastly covered with large leaves; the frame is placed in the "nursery", sheltered from the rays of the sun. After some weeks the

Left: The seedlings — each already with a couple of leaves — are removed from their wooden germinating trays. wrapped in small bags. and kept in the nursery until at least 6 pairs of leaves have sprouted on them. after which they are transplanted in their definitive locations. *Above:* A new plantation on the plain of Antigua (Guatemala). The small plants are about a year old. The distance between them is very carefully measured to permit enough harvesting and maintenance space when the plants are 3-4 years old.

seedlings appear above the soil and grow the first pair of leaves, whilst below the surface a root system extending for about a dozen centimetres has already developed. The method of propagating from cuttings on the other hand is done by taking pieces of branch from the adult plant, taking care to select only unblemished branches and those not too close to the trunk, so that they are not too large in diameter. The branches are cut into sections about 10 centimetres long, each section having a pair of leaves; the sections are then cut in half lengthwise, and the leaf remaining on each piece is partially pruned. At this stage the cuttings are placed in a bed of soil as described above, with the leaf part uppermost, protruding above the soil. They are then given a good watering and the frames are placed in the "nursery" where after a few weeks' care the first roots appear, followed by the first leaves.

From this point onwards the two methods take the same course: before the roots become too big the growing plants are gently lifted and transplanted into individual bags (generally plastic) filled with good soil.

For almost a year the young plants remain in the "nursery" in their bags, and are given expert daily inspection.

When the sixth pair of leaves has formed and before the branches have developed, the young plants are finally planted out in the soil that has been well broken up and fertilized. Each plant is placed in a prepared hole together with all the soil in the bag, well irrigated and protected from the sun with large leaves. It takes three or four years before the plant begins to give a normal crop, and it is only after ten years that it reaches maximum productivity which, if other trunks do not develop from the primary root-stock, will start to decrease after about twenty years.

Life in the plantations: the coffee crop

The coffee plant grows in countries that lie between the two Tropics, in zones where there are no seasonal climatic changes: there it is always summer or something betwixt spring and summer.

Plants are therefore evergreen and bear fruit in a continuous cycle. Coffee plants are no exception and, lacking rising spring temperatures to prompt flowering, as is the case with plants in our part of the world, they depend on rainfall to this end. This means that following every rainfall, after about two weeks the plant will flower: if it rains ten times in a year, the

Right: Another Antigua plantation where highest-quality "washed" Arabica coffee is produced. Special trees not only protect the coffee plants from the constant wind caused by the hot slopes of the volcanoes, but also from the freezing air temperatures and overexposure to the sun's rays. The widely-extending roots of the trees also hold the soil firmly in place against rain erosion. All the precious coffee plants have to receive just the right amount of water, light and air.

plant will flower ten times. This explains the importance of climate and of rainfall in particular to the cultivation of coffee; it also explains why several weeks' drought in Brazil at a time when rains are normally expected can cause coffee prices to rise all over the world.

In some countries, such as Brazil and monsoon countries, rainfall is concentrated in certain months of the year. In others, rain may fall at any time. The importance of this factor is easily understood: after flowering, it takes Robusta 9 to 11 weeks and Arabica 6 to 8 weeks before the fruit is fully ripe.

So if the rainfall is distributed throughout the year, you find plants simultaneously bearing flowers, ripening fruit and fully ripe fruit.

This means that there are as many crops as there have been flowerings, so the rainfall influences not only the quantity of the harvest but also the regularity with which the fruit comes to maturity.

This in turn affects the growers in their choice of the most suitable method of harvesting.

After the flowering period, which lasts only a few days, the ovary of the fertilized flower rapidly develops into a fruit that is initially green in colour; by 6-10 weeks the berry has already reached its full size.

During the final weeks the berries change colour, becoming first yellow and eventually bright red, with the exception of a few varieties such as Bourbon whose ripe fruits are yellow. If they are not harvested at this stage, the drupes become garnet-red and then brown, while the pulp and the skin dry out and become hard; sometimes they fall to the ground. At times when the market is depressed this is the most economical way of harvesting in certain countries: the dry berries are simply gathered from the ground where they have fallen.

Above: Newly-sprouted seedlings in their soft, nutritious, nursery bed. The berries – which provide the initial nutriment – are still attached to the stems. After a few weeks, when the roots have developed, the spent berries become detached. *Right:* The branch of a coffee plant showing the various growth stages, from the bud to the ripe berry. Tropical weather remains fairly unchanged, so the plants have to rely on another signal to bud. In fact, the plants sprout new buds about 15 days after each heavy rainfall.

Above: The flowering period lasts just a few days. during which the bud opens. blooms. develops pollen and drops off the plant. The blossom's strong fragrance attracts hordes of insects, but the *Coffea arabica* plant is autogamous and needs no help with its pollination. *Right:* Coffee plantation in Kenya. The sight and fragrance that meet the senses when walking through a flowering coffee grove is enough to make one's head swim. The plants look snow-covered. and the spectacular colour contrast is heightened by the perfume-laden air.

At the opposite extreme there is the most painstaking and expensive method of harvesting, i.e. picking. This entails passing repeatedly among the plants at intervals of a few weeks, handpicking only the red berries, leaving the others to continue ripening. This is the method used in countries that produce coffee of the Arabica species and are more particular about the quality of their crop.

Another quite common method, especially in countries where the rainfall is concentrated at particular times of the year, is stripping. This means waiting until most of the drupes are ripe before harvesting, when all the berries are stripped from the

Preceding pages: The typical, soft-rolling hills of the Brazilian coffee-growing areas. Here we see Poços de Caldas, famous for the quality of its Santos. *Above:* Men and women picking coffee berries. *Right:* This same picking method is also used in Guatemala. Here we see the hand grasping the branch and the fingers detaching the ripe (red) berries and letting them fall into the basket. The green and yellow ones are left on the branches a little longer (one or two weeks) to properly ripen. The plants have to be gone over each time new berries ripen.

branches at the same time. This is done by grasping the branch at a point close to the trunk and drawing the hand down the branch, stripping off the berries which are allowed to fall into baskets or onto the ground to be collected later. Unfortunately this practice, which is fairly widespread, can lead to the pulp of the fruit being contaminated by the microbes, bacteria and fungi present in the soil, often causing fermentation or other forms of infestation that can affect the beans.

In various countries and in Brazil in particular men have long tried to mechanize the harvesting of coffee.

They have invented machines with two special vertical large "brushes" that, by rotating in opposite directions, strip the fruit from the branches, together with a lot of leaves. At present these machines are employed only in a few slightly undulating areas; their use is restricted because of the damage they do to the plants. Only the handpicking method guarantees that all the berries are perfectly ripe; with the stripping method or the mechanical method, the berries are not all equally ripe. This means that whilst most of the berries are fully ripe, there is always a greater or lesser percentage that is under-ripe or over-ripe, which gives rise to two kinds of problems. The first stems from the fact

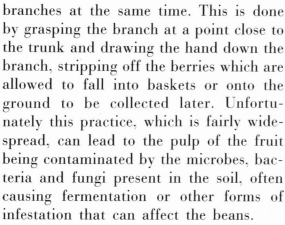

Above: The use of the stripping method in harvesting berries is done in Brazil and other countries that produce "natural" coffee. The branches are grasped near the main stem of the plant, and all the berries are stripped off and allowed to fall onto the ground. The berries are subsequently scooped up and put through a round sieve (*right*) to remove the leaves and the soil. The stripping method can only be used in places where flowering periods are closer together, such as where the climate is more variable with the change of seasons or where the rains are concentrated in certain periods of the year. Of course, with this method, there is no ripeness uniformity and the berries have to be sorted.

Above: Sacks full of berries being taken from a Kenya plantation to the processing area. Any type of vehicle will do for this job, as long as it covers the distance in a short time. If there is too long a delay, pulp fermentation will begin and will thus hurt the quality of the coffee. Before processing begins, all the unripe berries are removed. *Right:* The whole local population takes part in this work.

that the percentage of imperfectly ripe berries is variable: the flavour of different consignments, even though they come from neighbouring areas and from plants of the same species and variety, can differ according to the quantity of imperfect beans they contain. The second problem is connected with the increased likelihood of finding rotten fruit among over-ripe berries.

Whilst the problem caused by under-ripe fruit is "only" that the coffee is sharper and more bitter and noticeably less aromatic, rotten fruit can cause a very unpleasant smell when there is a "stinker" that can contaminate hundreds of other beans.

Fortunately during the last few decades electronic sorting machines have been perfected, which can pick out and discard most of the imperfect berries which result from the increasing use of the "speedy" stripping method of harvesting.

The importance of the climate

The ideal habitat for coffee plants is in the band between the two Tropics, in three main large areas: Central South America, Central Africa and the zone comprising India, the Indonesian Islands and Papua-New Guinea. Whichever species the plants belong to, whether Arabica or Robusta, the first climatic enemy is frost which reaches different altitudes according to latitude: whereas at the Equator it is never found below 2500 metres, in zones close to the Tropics it is even found at altitudes of 100-200 metres.

The plantations in Kenya are located more than 2000 metres above sea level, where the slopes are often very steep and there are short, heavy rainfalls. Were it not for the special trees planted in the coffee groves, serious soil damage would result. The roots of the trees hold the soil in place; any soil washed away is replaced with refill soil. However, this is a problem which only concerns the Arabica coffee plantations located at high elevations.

Thus in countries close to the Equator we find coffee plantations even at altitudes above 2000 metres, whereas the nearer we go to the Tropics, the lower the altitudes are at which coffee plantations are found until we are close to sea level.

To decide which species is best suited for cultivation in a particular area two main factors have to be taken into account: altitude and temperature. Arabica plantations are found at altitudes above 900 metres and where the average temperature falls between 20 and 25 degrees; Robusta plantations do well at sea level and where average temperatures are higher, between 24 and 26 degrees.

For all coffee plants the average minimum temperature should not be lower than 15 degrees and the maximum temperature should not exceed 30 degrees. Rainfall is

also of vital importance: ideally there should be an annual rainfall of between 1500 and 2000 millimetres, while, if it is less than 1000 millimetres, coffee growing is almost impossible.

A medium humidity is ideal, and especially necessary in periods of drought to limit the amount of water lost by the plants through evaporation. A further consideration is exposure to the sun, which coffee plants like, but not for too many hours of the day. So that the plants do not get too much sun, a suitably shady slope is chosen, or else "shade trees" may be used: these are trees with a tall trunk and a broad umbrella of leaves which are planted among the coffee plants to give the right play of light and shade during the day. Shade trees can also be useful in protecting the plants from cold

The coffee plant's worst enemy is freezing weather, and temperatures even just a few degrees below freezing can cause serious damage. Continued exposure will cause loss of leaves and eventual death. *Above:* Trees in among the coffee plants, which provide short-term protection against freezing temperatures. The photo immediately above dramatically shows how there were not enough trees to protect these Guatamelan coffee plants from early-morning freezing damage caused by evaporating fog. The protective trees also require proper care in order to be effective.

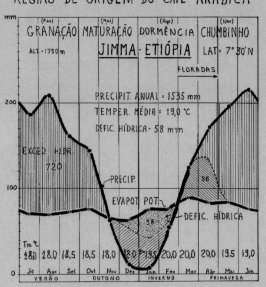

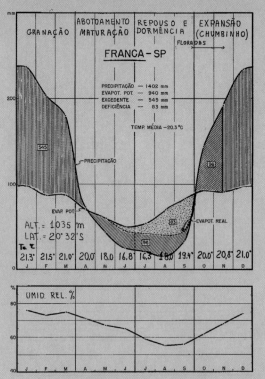

BALANÇO HÍDRICO CLIMÁTICO PELO MÉTODO DE "THORNTHWAITE & MATHER - 1955 -125mm" E MÉDIAS MENSAIS DA UMIDADE RELATIVA DO AR, PARA FRANCA - SP.

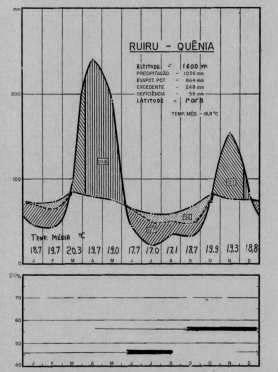

BALANÇO HÍDRICO CLIMÁTICO PELO MÉTODO DE "THORNTHWAITE & MATHER - 1955 -125mm" E MÉDIAS MENSAIS DA UMIDADE RELATIVA DO AR, PARA RUIRU - QUÊNIA.

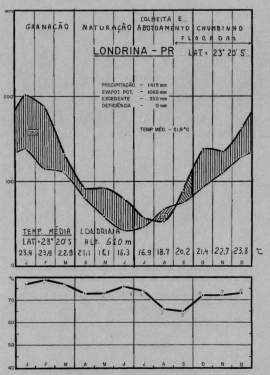

BALANÇO HÍDRICO CLIMÁTICO PELO MÉTODO DE "THORNTHWAITE & MATHER - 1955 -125mm" E MÉDIAS MENSAIS DA UMIDADE RELATIVA DO AR, PARA LONDRINA - PR.

and hoar-frost, but often they are not used because less sun means a poorer harvest. Lastly, wind must also be taken into account: the branches of the young plants are not very strong and may be damaged by strong winds, a factor which also governs the choice of zone suitable for coffee growing. In addition to climatic factors, the nature of the ground itself is a vital consideration: the earth must be fertile, deep and well-drained. The roots of the coffee plant extend for up to a metre and a half below ground, and the soil should preferably be slightly acid (pH between 5 and 6) and contain a balanced quantity of phosphor, potassium, calcium and magnesium. Organic or chemical fertilizers are used to compensate for any insufficiency. In short, a good plantation basically depends on the right choice of site and the best climatic conditions and soil, as there is a limit to what man can do to correct any of these.

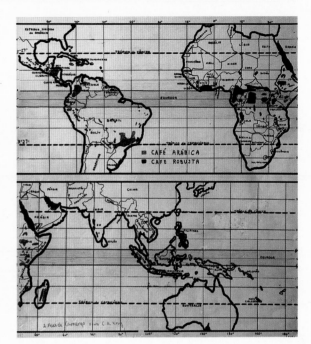

Coffee paradises
Coffee is a product of the earth and, as is always the case with the fruits of agriculture, its cultivation is influenced by — and influences in its turn — local culture and customs. So we cannot regard coffee growing as a single, homogeneous universal activity: in every country we find differences in the way in which coffee influences both economic and social life, in the species and variety of plants used, in the areas in which they are cultivated, in the methods of production, harvesting and processing.

To give an example of this diversity we have chosen three of the seven most important countries producing coffee of the most prized species: Arabica.

These countries are Brazil, Guatemala and Kenya.

Left: Curves showing average temperature and rainfall values for four production centres, with drought periods adversely affecting flowering and, if prolonged, the health of the plants themselves. *Above:* Main cultivation areas lying between the Tropics of Cancer and Capricorn. The Arabica species is cultivated at elevations exceeding 900 metres. The Robusta is more hardy and can be cultivated at sea level. The best climate for both is where the average temperatures range between 20 and 25°C and the yearly rainfall averages between 1,500 and 2,000 mm.

Brazil

The largest country in South America is also the world's leading coffee producer, its 20-30 million bags each year accounting for almost a third of world production. Coffee growing is of considerable importance to Brazil's economy, representing about 10 per cent of the gross national product and 20 per cent of the total value of its exports. Five million people are employed in the production of coffee from the 230,000 *fazendas* that cover more than two million hectares at altitudes between 2000 and 1000 metres. At present there are more than three thousand million plants, mainly of the Arabica species: the most common varieties are Bourbon, Typica, Mundo Novo, Catuai and Maragogype. Robusta production is called Conillon. As well as being great producers, the Brazilians are also great consumers of coffee: to make their famous *cafesiño* they consume 3.5 kg per head per year.

In keeping with the somewhat fatalistic philosophy of the Brazilian people, coffee growers use rather spartan methods and rarely try to combat or mitigate the effects of external circumstances. Thus we find that for many years they did not use nurseries to raise seedlings, but sowed seeds straight into the ground in the plan-

tations: of four seeds planted in each hole, at least one or two would germinate, but the percentage of success was left to chance. Today nurseries are common, but it is still only in the northern plantations that shade trees are used, although they would also be a great help in the south to protect the coffee plants from frost which frequently damages them.

Irrigation works are not common either and the quantity of the crop is therefore greatly affected by the amount of rainfall. New plants are pruned after six years, the trunk being cut back to a height of one metre and all secondary and tertiary bran-

Preceding pages: Coffee plants stretch out of sight on the Minas Gerais hills in Brazil. *Left:* The entrance of a Brazilian "fazenda" – near Poços de Caldas – where the "green gold" is produced. *Above:* The first step in setting up a new plantation is to cut down and burn all the trees.

ches being removed; this operation is repeated every three years instead of more frequent and less radical pruning. Because the flowerings are concentrated in the months from August to November, the least costly and fastest stripping method can be used for harvesting, which falls in the period between May and August. The berries are stripped from the branches and allowed to fall to the ground, and are afterwards collected for processing.

The dry method is the preferred method of processing and also the most economical one. It is therefore not surprising that Brazilian production varies greatly from year to year both in quantity (from 14 to 40 million bags) and quality. Nonetheless

the best Brazilian coffees – Santos from the hills of Mogiana and Washed Bahia (processed by the "wet" method) from the region of the same name – are unbeatable for their flavour, body and aroma and form the ideal basis for the blends suitable for making espresso coffee.

Guatemala

Whilst Brazil is noted both for the quantity and quality of its coffee production, Guatemala coffee is famed simply for its excellent quality. Average annual production in fact amounts only to 2.5 million bags, almost exclusively of the Bourbon, Typica and Maragogype varieties of Arabica. Even so, coffee still represents about a third of the total value of the country's exports and employs almost a third of the population. Guatemala's 64,000 plantations occupy about 240,000 hectares at altitudes even above two thousand metres, on quite steep slopes. They are almost always protected by shade trees, that ensure the right amount of exposure to the sun and afford protection against frost. There are several nurseries where the best seeds are selected and the seedlings raised for the first year. The fruit-bearing plants are pruned using a technique that allows several trunks to grow from the same rootstock, thereby

Above: After harvesting, the berries are allowed to dry in the sun right there on the plantation. The dried berries – now in the so-called "coco" condition – are then transferred to the processing plants where they are given the "beneficiamento" treatment (pulp removal). *Right above:* First thing in the morning, the plantation tools are unloaded from the trucks; in the evening the same trucks are loaded with the fruit of the day's labour.

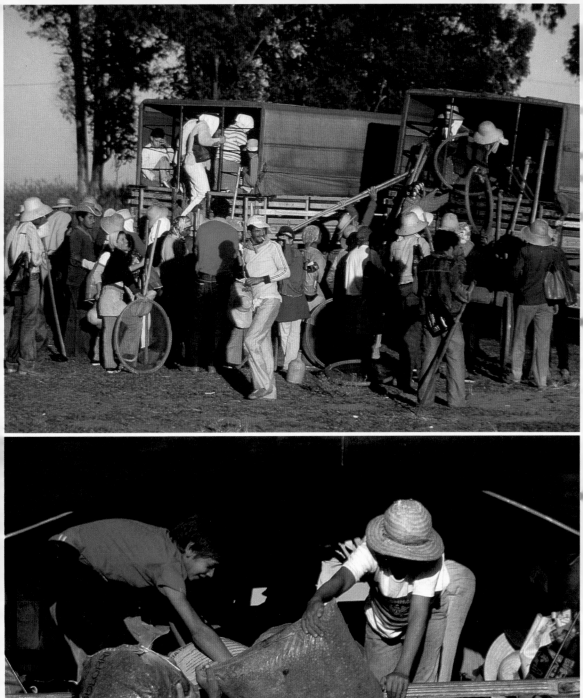

maintaining both high productivity and quality for many years. Irrigation is not necessary because there is sufficient rainfall, concentrated in the months from January to March.

Harvesting takes place between November and April, using the handpicking method which guarantees that all the berries are of the desired degree of ripeness. The most commonly used method of processing them is the expensive "wet" process. Only the larger *haciendas* have their own machines and equipment; the small *fincas* depend on the *beneficiamento* centres scattered among the hundreds of small pieces of land. Such punctilious care is taken during processing that the beans are still protected by their parchment until they are to be packed for shipping: it is only then that they are hulled and polished to remove the brittle parchment and silver skin. The result of such careful processing is the Guatemala S.H.B. (strictly hard bean) from the centres of Coban, Antigua and Atitlan: a high-quality very mild coffee, not bitter, of average acidity and with a good body, characterised by a strong aroma which varies from chocolatey to flowery. It is ideal for espresso coffee blends and is one of the most favoured components in blends for percolated coffee.

Kenya

The "Switzerland of Africa", as Kenya is often described, is also famous for the quality of its coffee (of which it produces only one and a half million bags a year). Its mild and settled climate is as ideal for man as it is for coffee plants of the Arabica species, of which the Bourbon and Kent varieties are cultivated from 1500 to 2100 metres above sea level. Even at these altitudes the plants are never touched by frost.

To guarantee the correct amount of water, many plantations have irrigation systems, and shade trees, generally bananas, are

Left: Guatemalan children among the lush coffee plants smile for the photographer. The branches bend earthward under the weight of the berries. When the berries ripen, these children will also help in the harvest. *Above:* Small quantities of berries being taken to the processing centre. In Guatemala, only the most important "haciendas" can afford to have their own expensive bean-processing equipment.

used to regulate the amount of the sun. There are about 300,000 plantations, grouped in 150 cooperatives: direct private ownership is not allowed and the State is very active in coordinating and supporting the work of the coffee growers, and in other ways. It has established research centres to select seeds and combat the diseases and parasites that affect the plants, and through these centres it gives continual assistance to the cooperatives.

In Kenya too pruning is done in a manner that makes it possible to grow several trunks from the same rootstock, which means that today there are fully productive plants whose rootstock goes back to the first decade of the century.

There are two flowering periods: October and November and from March to May, although minor flowerings are possible throughout the year. Harvesting is thus carried out weekly, using the handpicking method, but is concentrated mainly in June-September and above all October-January, when almost 80 per cent of the total crop is gathered.

The "wet" process is the one most favoured, and is generally carried out on the farms themselves.

The coffee beans, still in their parchment, are then transported to the processing centre in Nairobi, the capital, where the beans are hulled and polished.

Each consignment is taken over by the State and then sold at auction to authorized exporters (of whom there are only a few dozen). The producers are paid in accordance with the price fetched at auction, so there is a strong incentive to produce coffee of the highest quality. This is why Kenya coffee appears on the international markets at distinctly higher than average prices.

The best Kenya coffee is the double A (AA indicates the larger size of the bean): it makes a very mild coffee, not bitter, with high acidity and average body: it has a strong aroma, flowery and even fruity, that sometimes evokes the aroma of toasted bread. Kenya coffee is used above all in percolated-coffee blends; even a small percentage added to espresso coffee blends will lend them a touch of their characteristic aroma. Large quantities cannot be used because of the pronounced acidity. Contrary to the inhabitants of Brazil and Guatemala, Kenyans prefer tea to coffee, consuming only 200 grams of coffee per head per year: almost their entire production is therefore destined for export, and represents about a third of the total value of exports.

Preceding pages: The market in Antigua, Guatemala, has a wide variety of products, mostly fruit and vegetables. *Right:* A plantation in Kenya. Initial depulping, fermentation, washing and drying of the beans right after harvesting are carried out in the middle of the plantation.

THE
PROCESSING
OF
COFFEE

Weighing, hulling and discarding

Only the seeds of the fruits of the coffee plant can be used for human consumption, for making the aromatic beverage. Once these small nuts (the coffee beans) have been extracted, the rest of the berry is discarded, and generally used as fertilizer. The simplest method for extracting the beans is that suggested by nature: if the ripe berry is left on the branch, it will begin to dry out and after a few weeks will probably fall to the ground, where the process continues for some weeks longer. If the berries are collected at this stage, the skin and the pulp are dry, and the beans can be extracted by splitting the outer skin, parchment included.

This was certainly the method used by the Arabs since the discovery of coffee, but it was the Dutch who classified it as OIB, Oost Indische Bereiding, or the East Indies method, after introducing harvesting in place of leaving the fruit to fall to the ground naturally. The method is still used in countries that have a dry climate at harvest time. Coffee berries take up to 20 days to dry out, during which time they are spread out in the open air: so it must not rain and there should not be much humidity. These climatic conditions are not found in the West Indies so there the Dutch, apparently as early as 1740, introduced the WIB method (West Indische Bereiding), which consisted of stoning the berries after harvesting to remove the beans from the skin and the pulp, thereby accelerating the drying process. This method was adopted above all in Java, where to this day consignments of coffee treated in this way are marked WIB. Removed from the pulp, the beans are nevertheless still covered in a jelly-like substance insoluble in water which quickly causes the beans to go rotten; this has to be removed before drying the beans. The Dutch realised that a slight fermentation of this mucilage, which took place spontaneously if the beans were heaped up, would decompose and loosen it so that it could be washed off. This method is also used today and is known as the wet process, while the natural method is also known as the dry method. These are the only methods of processing coffee used today.

Wet process

For the process it is essential that the coffee berries are harvested by handpicking: the berries must all be at the desired stage of ripeness, so that the pulp is soft and the beans easily extracted. They should also all be of the same size, because

Facing title: Women working among the sacks. Most of the workers on coffee plantations are women and children. *Right:* Before being "wet"-processed, all the unripe berries are sorted out because these can cause processing difficulties and can lower the quality of the final product.

Left: In Kenya the berries are transported in bulk form and unloaded by means of shovels. *Upper top:* Sacks of berries being unloaded at a processing center in Guatemala. *Upper bottom:* Berries being emptied from the sacks into vats that feed the depulping machines; depulping is the first step in the long "wet" process. and assures product homogeneity.

any smaller berries would escape having their pulp removed. Lastly there must be no foreign bodies, particularly stones which could wreck the machines. After very careful picking, the berries are generally weighed and inspected, to eliminate any that are unripe or imperfect. Sometimes they are washed and sorted according to their gravity in water: those that float are discarded together with any stones, leaves and bits of wood. The discarded berries are generally used for consignments of inferior quality: in Kenya for example they are processed by the dry method and the poorer quality coffee thus obtained is called Mbuni.

The berries are now ready for the pulp to be removed, which may be done by machines with rotating drums or discs. In either case the berry is squeezed between the rotating part and a fixed blade until the skin splits, liberating the two beans still covered by the parchment and the jelly-like mucilage; the beans and the pulp are separated by the machine itself. The gap between the blade and the rotating parts is adjusted according to the size of the berries: if the gap is too wide the pulp will not be removed, and if it is not wide enough the parchment may be broken and the beans damaged. Calibration is a delicate operation done by trial and error: this explains the importance of having berries that are all the same size.

After the pulp has been removed the beans have to go through the process of sieving and washing. Both these processes serve to remove any remaining pulp and skin: the first is done by using a sieve designed to retain only the beans. Washing may be done either in running water, passing the beans back and forth along a labyrinth of washing canals, or in large tanks in which the beans are repeatedly stirred.

Fermentation, washing, drying
In order to dry the beans in the parchment, the layer of mucilage, 0.5-2 millimetres thick, which coats them, must first be removed.

This layer is composed of substances that are insoluble in water and if it is not removed it can cause the beans to ferment and stick together while drying.

Fortunately slight fermentation causes the mucilage to dissolve, so leaving the parchment smooth and clean. This can be achieved in two ways: by immersion in water, or else by the wet method which means taking advantage of the moisture in the mucilage itself without adding water. In both cases the beans are put into tanks

Preceding pages: A plantation in Kenya in full bloom. The main blooming periods in this country are October and November, and from March to May.
Right: Unripe or defective berries are not wet-processed, but are removed and allowed to dry in the sun. The product obtained is of medium-to-low quality and is usually only for local consumption.

Above: The manually-operated depulper removes the beans from the rest of the berries (shell and pulp). This operation, in addition to the subsequent fermentation and washing phases, requires the use of a considerable amount of water. *Inset:* Beans still covered with their thin membranes (parchment), which come off during final processing. *Right:* The enzymes in this fermentation vat dissolve the mucilage that covers the bean skins.

In Guatemala, the beans with their skins on are allowed to dry in the sun. This is better than machine-processing because better quality is obtained.

Top left: The "gold" (so called because of the colour of the beans) is continually agitated by mechanical means to facilitate drying. *Top right:* Reject berries being sun-dried on grates before undergoing dry processing. *Bottom:* The berries, first after two days in the sun and then after about ten days in the sun.

with cement walls, a little over a metre deep. With the first method water is added to cover the beans, but in other respects the methods are the same.

Fermentation starts spontaneously, but is often helped by adding certain enzymes or else by simply adding water from tubs in which fermentation is already well advanced. The sole purpose of fermentation is to eliminate the unwanted mucilage, which can take from a minimum of 6 hours to a maximum of 80, according to the external temperature and the thickness and composition of the mucilage. Fermentation without adding water is the quicker

method: in either case the beans must be stirred frequently to promote simultaneous chemical reactions. These cause both an increase of temperature in the tank and an increase in acidity, from a pH of almost 7 to about 4.5, the value at which the enzymes have difficulty in carrying out their activity.

But by this time fermentation is at its final stage and the mucilage has dissolved, so that it can be easily and completely removed by thorough and repeated washing.

Like the pre-fermentation washings, these may also be carried out either in the tanks themselves or in a system of water canals, or else by special machines. Water is not always available in the quantity necessary for the wet process (it requires about 100-120 litres for each kilo of coffee) so it often has to be recycled. There are no problems up to four recyclings; above this number an acid called propionic acid develops, which gives the coffee a disagreeable aroma of onions.

A final sorting is done during the wet process: any beans that float to the surface are discarded. This work is facilitated by the fact that the beans are driven along the square-sided water canals until they reach the drying area: beans that float travel

Left: In the washing phase, the beans are carried along large concrete troughs. Special wooden poles are used to help move the beans along. *Above:* After washing, sieves are used to remove the beans. *Below:* The beans are subsequently spread out to dry in the sun, weather permitting.

more quickly on the surface. In addition to the methods described above, there are two other methods, not much used, of eliminating the mucilage: the alkaline method, quite common only in Brazil, and the mechanical method, specially developed in Indonesia.

When the final washing is completed, the beans in their parchment must be dried: in fact they contain over 50 per cent moisture, which must be brought down to about 12 per cent.

The drying process is, or ought to be, quicker than drying the whole berry and the main advantage lies in the fact that it can be interrupted without risk of unwanted fermentation. Drying may be done naturally, by spreading out the beans on

Above: Berries sun-drying in Brazil. where the dry process is used most prevalently. The beans are generally spread right out on the bare ground. but sometimes they are spread on a concrete surface. *Right:* In Kenya the beans with their skins on are placed on grates that are raised off the ground. Since the layer of beans is not thick. only a few mixing operations are required during the drying period.

wickerwork racks or on cement threshing floors, or in drying machines.

The natural drying process is considered better for the quality of the coffee and is therefore used in preference, providing weather conditions permit. In this case, especially during the first stage before the parchment has dried, the beans are frequently turned. In all, the natural drying process takes from 1 to 3 weeks: if it rains during this time, the beans may be temporarily protected with waterproof sheets or moved under cover until the sun returns.

The dried beans – still with their skins on – are then sacked and stored in the warehouse. To safeguard final product quality, the warehouse – as well as the fermentation and washing sections – provides plenty of ventilation and shade. In Guatemala, the practice is to provide maximum natural protection for the beans by leaving their skins on right up to the time they are delivered to the dock.

When drying is complete the beans in their parchment are put into bags and transported to processing centres or warehouses where (either at once or prior to shipping) they go through one final process to remove the parchment, which is called decortication. As we have seen, the wet process is quite complex and requires large quantities of water (but it is used in countries where the climate is not dry enough to use the dry or natural method). However, coffee processed by the wet method is considered to be of higher quality than coffee processed by the natural or dry method and its market price is therefore higher. This is due not so much to any technical superiority of the wet process, as to the opportunity it affords of sorting the berries and beans at almost every stage, so that any imperfect ones are discarded. From the chemical viewpoint, the most obvious difference is in the fermentation which seems to be lacking in the dry process. This is only an apparent difference, because as the berries dry fermentation does start in the pulp but then stops through lack of water. The main advantage of washed coffees is therefore the absence or almost total absence of imperfect beans, which makes for coffee of dependably high quality.

Dry processing: drying in the sun

As we have already seen, the dry method of removing coffee beans is the most ancient, because it is what occurs naturally if the berries are not harvested when they are fully ripe. After this stage in fact the berries become darker in colour and start to dry out, as happens to the shell of walnuts.

In some cases the fruit falls to the ground of its own accord, where it continues to dry out; otherwhise it remains attached to the plant until it is quite dry. So it might be thought that the simplest method would be to collect the dry berries from the ground

Dry-processed coffee undergoes less sorting both before and after processing. Therefore. after the beans have been separated from their dried shells. the heavy and light foreign material has to be sorted out. This includes pieces of berry material. bean skins. wood. leaves. etc.. as well as stones. gravel and bits of metal. *Above:* A special. weight-sensitive sorting machine for removing this foreign material.

Above: The sacks (usually made of hemp) are first prepared and filled with coffee beans. *Side:* The filled sacks are then sewn closed by means of a special sewing machine. The weight of a standard loaded sack is 60 kg. although the 70 kg and 80 kg standard weights are also used by some producers. *Right:* Sacked, raw beans ready for shipment. A few months storage helps to stabilize the quality.

or the plants and then extract the beans, leaving the job of drying to nature.

This alas is not the case: berries left on the branches, especially in hot sun, tend to ferment and may produce nasty-smelling beans known as stinkers.

It is even worse if the berries fall to the ground: the bacteria and fungi present in the soil can infest the berry, helped in this by any rainfall. It seems that one of the most serious defects of coffee, the Rio taste (which is like the smell of medicines), is in fact due to the activity of the enzymes of a fungus which spreads into the pulp of the berry if it is left lying on the ground for long.

Man must therefore take charge of the drying process, after picking berries at the desired stage of ripeness, or at the least picking them before they are over-ripe. In fact whereas the delicate machines used to remove the pulp in the wet process require berries that are all fully ripe, with the dry method the presence of berries that are not fully ripe does not prove an obstacle. So it is easy to understand why in countries that use this simpler process, the preferred method of harvesting is stripping, which does not take into account the degree of ripeness of individual berries. However the presence of unripe berries compromises the

quality of the consignment of coffee, so the best producers sort the berries prior to drying.

One of the simplest and most efficient methods is to put the berries in large tanks of water and, by means of a tube immersed halfway, to select only the berries that have a slightly higher specific weight, which are the ripe berries. Any dry ones will float, and unripe berries will sink to the bottom: both are discarded.

Drying can be done naturally, in the sun, or else by machine. The second method is more expensive and is therefore only used in cases of necessity, if there is too much humidity in the air. To dry them naturally, the berries are spread out no more than 5-6 centimetres deep in the wickerwork racks or more often on the threshing floor, probably paved with stones or cement. They must be turned several times a day, to promote water evaporation and prevent any large-scale fermentation from starting, which would compromise the quality of the coffee.

This work can be done manually or with the help of tractors; it is worth pointing out that for every thousand plants a drying surface of 50 square metres is necessary, and in large plantations thousands of plants are cultivated: for 200,000 plants a

Right: Two photos taken in Brazil, where the berries are normally dry-processed.
Above: A tractor is used to mix the berries spread out on the ground to dry.
Below: Manual mixing with the use of simple wooden tools. Mixing is required to assure uniform drying and prevent fermentation.

drying area larger than a football pitch is required!

The drying process can take up to 20 days; if it rains during this period the berries have to be covered with plastic sheets or moved under cover. The same is also done at night, so that the humidity is not re-absorbed by the pulp and mucilage which are very hygroscopic at the drying stage. The dry berry is smaller than when it was picked, its colour is dark brown and its moisture content is about 13 per cent.

From processing to the bag

To free the beans from the pod consisting of skin, dried pulp and mucilage and the parchment, costly decorticating machines are needed. Growers rarely have their own; usually the dry berries are transported to processing centres available to producers over wide areas and often run by cooperatives. Here the machines break the dry pod, separating it from the beans. Contrary to coffee berries processed by the wet method, those that have been pro-cessed by the dry method retain the silver skin that adheres to the beans; the colour of the skin is used as a guide to sorting out possibly imperfect beans. There are generally large quantities of these at this stage.

In fact a whole series of sorting processes is necessary, in the devising of which man's imagination has been given full rein. They range from the use of forced air currents to separate the remains of the pod and the empty beans from the healthy ones, to the use of vibrating sloping surfaces to separate the flat beans from the "pea-berry" or rounded beans; from sifting machines that sort the beans according to size, to optical sorting machines that will discard beans of defective colour.

Sometimes defective beans are picked out by hand: the beans are carried out by conveyor belt past the sorters whose job is to spot and discard any imperfect beans.

Modern electronic sorting machines, with highly sensitive photoelectric cells, are not only much faster but also much more accurate, and so are replacing manual labour. There are several types of ma-chines: the simplest are monochromatic, and basically measure the amount of light reflected by each bean as it passes in front of the photoelectric cells, discarding those that reflect too much (the white ones) or too little (the black ones). The more sophisticated machines are bichromatic, able to analyse two colours, generally green and red.

In this case electronics makes it possible to

Left: Coffee beans being transported from Brazilian plantations to the Guaxupe plant to undergo various sorting operations. including sorting by weight (to remove foreign material). sorting by colour (to remove bad beans). and sorting by size (to separate the beans according to their size). Sorting is of prime importance. especially as regards dry-processed ("natural") beans.

sort out the beans on the basis of ratio thresholds between two colours or of still more complex parameters, so that not only white or black beans are discarded but also those of certain shades of green that often indicate much more serious defects from the point of view of taste and smell.

Lastly there are sorting machines with ultra-violet rays that make use of the principle of fluorescence, whose photo-electric cells are able to pick out beans in which a process of fermentation has started but which have not yet undergone any change in colour.

The various sorting operations play a particularly important role for coffee processed by the dry method, as they are concentrated at the beginning and above all at the end of the whole processing cycle: it is at this stage that good natural coffees are made, by paying the closest attention to the elimination of imperfect beans.

Now the coffee beans are ready for weighing and packing in the bags of jute or sisal (generally 60 kg bags, but even up to 100 kg) in which they will travel to their destination.

Classification

The best way of judging the quality of a consignment of coffee is to take a sample, roast it, make it into a drink and taste it. This is the only way of telling how all the factors which affect its taste, from the species of plant to the method of processing, and from the country of origin to production techniques, have interacted together.

There are so many variables that it would be impossible to describe them all. Nevertheless each consignment is labelled with a brief description which gives buyers some idea, without actually "seeing" the bags, of the type of coffee and its value on the market. Each producing country has its own method of classification: some items of information are always given, such as place of origin sometimes accompanied by region or centre of production

Above: Workers picking out the bad beans according to colour as the beans are carried along on a conveyor belt. *Right (top to bottom and left to right):* Checking samples to verify correct machine screening; bean conveyor from one machine to next; inclined-plane machine for separating flat from oval-shaped beans; electronic machine for colour sorting; after sorting, the lot is classified by an expert.

(e.g. Colombia, Armenia) or port of embarkation.

Other essential items of information are the species of plant (Arabica or Robusta) and type of processing (natural or wet); these items are often understood without being specified, as in the case of a country producing mainly one species or using one processing system. Thus it is not necessary to specify that Santos is natural nor that it is Arabica: on the other hand it is stated that Bahia is washed; by Costa Rica it is understood that it is a washed Arabica; but if the coffee comes from the Cameroons, which produces both species and uses both methods of processing, all details are specified.

There is also usually an indication of sieve size, or the diameter of the hole through which the bean will pass, which is generally expressed in sixty-fourths of an inch: the values go from 13 to 20. This is the system used by the Brazilians, whereas many other countries use the classifications AA-A-B-C to indicate in decreasing order the size of Arabica beans and Grades I-II-III for Robusta: Grade I corresponds to AA or a sieve size 16-18, equal to 7.2 millimetres. If the beans are pea-berry this is specified, otherwise it means that the beans are flat beans.

Another important piece of data is the percentage of imperfect beans, usually expressed in accordance with the New York Coffee and Sugar Exchange method: NY2 means that there are 4 imperfect beans in every 300 grams; NY3 that there are 12 and so on up to NY8.

A black bean equals one imperfect, but it takes five unripe or five broken to add up to one imperfect.

This method does not always attribute values that are consistent with taste and aroma of the coffee, giving for example great importance to its appearance and to the presence of foreign bodies that are easily removed.

Sometimes the crop from which the consignment comes is also specified: "new crop" if from the most recent, "old crop" if from the previous crop.

Other classifications used in Central America take into account the density of the beans: H.B. and S.H.B. mean Hard Bean and Strictly Hard Bean: the markings also signify that the plantation is situated above an altitude of 1600 metres. Other factors can also feature in the classification: the Brazilians are the most specific and may also describe the colour, the method of roasting and the kind of coffee the beans will make.

Left (top to bottom and left to right): The most common defects found in raw coffee beans: unripe beans; fermented beans; damaged beans; "shell"-shaped beans; bits of wood; whitish beans; black beans; beans with skins on (considered defects here); bits of outer skin. Each lot is classified according to the defects, each one being rated according to its seriousness.

Left: Going home after a day's work on a plantation in Antigua. *Top:* Two views of the market in Antigua. Guatemala. *Above left:* Native women at the Misarara market in Kenya. *Above right:* There is no skimping on barbed wire. and armed guards in Antigua protect the so-called "gold" (beans with skins on).

WORLD · GREEN · COFFEE TRADE

In coffee circles the world is conventionally divided in two: producers on the one hand and consumers on the other. By "consumer" what is meant is a country that does not produce coffee but is solely a consumer, whereas producing countries are also consumers, and in fact annually consume on average almost 20 million bags (of 60 kg) out of the total of 90-100 million bags produced.

The international coffee trade is regulated by the ICO, International Coffee Organiza-tion, to which belong fifty-odd producing countries that represent about 98 per cent of the world crop, and the principal consumer countries of the Western world. The organisation does not however include about twenty minor producers, whose crop often amounts to some tens of thousands of bags, and the consumer countries of the Warsaw Pact, Israel and a few others.

The group of consumer countries who are members of the ICO annually consume about 55 million bags, and non-member countries about a dozen.

The ICO has subdivided the producers into four groups, according to the similarity in quality of their produce: Colombian Mild, to which belong Colombia, Kenya and Tanzania; Brazilian and other Arabicas, which groups together Brazil and Ethiopia; Other Milds, to which belong all the other producers of Arabica, and lastly Robusta, which groups together all the producers of this species.

The principal objectives of the ICO are on the one hand to increase world consumption of coffee and on the other hand to stabilize equitable prices for the producers. To the latter end the members of the organisation have signed an agreement renewable on a four-year basis (the ICA - International Coffee Agreement) to fix the

Facing title: Two coffee experts of a Brazilian exporting firm classify the grain size, defects and final in-cup results of various lots. *Above:* The official Santos Coffee Exchange quotations are marked in white chalk on the quotation board. *Right:* The important dates concerning Brazilian coffee history are noted in the inscription on the outside of the Exchange (founded in 1917).

82

1727 — COFFEA BRASILIAE FULCRUM — 1927

A COMMISSÃO CENTRAL
DO
2° CENTENARIO DO CAFÉ
EM NOME DA LAVOURA PAULISTA

HOMENAGEM
AO COMMERCIO DE SANTOS

TRABALHO — PROBIDADE
COHESÃO — CIVISMO

1797   PRIMEIRAS EXPORTAÇÕES DE CAFÉ
1850/51 EXPORTAÇÃO DIRECTA PARA O EXTRANGEIRO
                                    103.260 Sᴬ
1906/07 EXPORTAÇÃO MAXIMA   13.874.113 Sᴬ

1870   FUNDAÇÃO DA ASSOCIAÇÃO COMMERCIAL
       1ᵃ EXPOSIÇÃO DE CAFÉ EM S. LUIZ
1904   COM O CONCURSO DA PRAÇA DE SANTOS
1917   INAUGURAÇÃO DA BOLSA DO CAFÉ

export quota for each coffee-producing country and also to fix two price levels (minimum and maximum) between which average prices can fluctuate. Prices are taken daily at the London and Paris-Le Havre markets for the Robusta and at the New York Market for the Arabica, in accordance with the four groups already mentioned.

If prices over a fortnight fall below the minimum threshold, the export quotas are reduced; if they rise above the maximum the export quotas are increased, or stopped altogether if prices continue to rise steadily over a long period. This arrangement

prevents prices from falling too low in periods of over-production, but it cannot prevent prices from rising when there is a crop shortage.

In practice the coffee trade is between the exporter, who obtains consignments from the growers, often with the State as intermediary, and the coffee-roasting firms, located in the importing countries. Between the exporter and the roaster we generally find an intermediary, either a row-coffee dealer who acquires the consignments and sells them in his turn to one or more coffee-roasting firms (usually average to small businesses), generally splitting up the consignments, or else a broker. In the second case the buying and selling is done directly and the broker takes a commission for acting as intermediary. The number of exporters is limited by the producing countries by means of issuing a limited number of export licenses, but there is no corresponding limitation in consumer countries with regard to importing coffee.

Expert tasting

Contracts of sale and purchase of coffee consignments, agreed between exporters and dealers or roasters, contain first and foremost information about the type of

Preceding pages: The trading room of the Santos Exchange. where Brazilian coffee is bought and sold at prices that regard a future delivery date. *Above:* Coffee tasters at work at the typical. round. rotating tasting table. The samples are normally prepared as infusions (brews). *Below:* The wherewithal for preparing a sample for the "espresso" method.

coffee in question, or a description. Then follow the price, conditions of payment, delivery and insurance. As the description, necessarily brief, can give only an approximate idea of the coffee in the consignments, the purchaser often also requests a sample for testing prior to concluding the deal. This allows him firstly to tell whether the quality suits his particular require-

ments and secondly to judge if the price is a fair one.

Since the most important qualities of coffee are the organoleptic ones, that is to say taste and smell, part of the sample, which usually weighs from 100 to 300 grams, is used to make test cups of coffee for tasting.

This operation requires a small coffee-

A group of tasters, using a so-called "goûte-café" (a specially-shaped spoon), taste samples taken from various lots and prepared both as brew and as "espresso". Each preparation highlights a particular taste or aroma. To avoid over-absorption of caffeine, the tasters do not swallow the coffee but spit it out into special basins after having tasted it.

roasting machine for roasting the sample, a coffee grinder and the equipment for making the beverage – usually very basic equipment as the most common system is simply to leave about 10 grams of ground coffee to infuse for about five minutes in 150 cc of boiling water.

As there is no standard procedure for tasting, the other aspects regarding the method of roasting the sample and grading the coffee vary from one country to another, with the result that there is not always agreement about the value of the coffee sampled. To taste the coffee a fairly deep roundish spoon is used, called a *goûte-café* by analogy with the sommelier's *taste-vin*.

The coffee is tasted without sugar, often at a revolving table which makes it easy to move from one cup to another; since the taster could not swallow dozens of sips of coffee, after tasting and noting the qualities of each he spits it out. The coffee is graded according to taste and aroma: the richest terminology for describing the latter is the Brazilian, but this is not adopted universally. In Italy, because of the popularity of coffee prepared by the espresso method, the samples for tasting are often prepared in the same way, to ensure that the consignment will be suitable. Tasting is generally carried out before the sale is concluded, or alternatively at a later stage if the contract contains the clause "subject to approval of sample", in which case, if the sample does not prove acceptable, the contract is cancelled. After tasting, the remainder of the sample is generally kept to check that it matches with the consignments on delivery. A specially equipped tasting room or laboratory is usually reserved for tasting samples and keeping records.

Sorting and blending

When a consignment of coffee reaches the coffee-roasting firm, whose job is to turn the green beans into the finished product ready for the consumer, it undergoes a

The "raw-bean" section of a coffee-roasting establishment. where all the overlooked foreign material and unsuitable beans are removed before the acceptable beans are sent to the roasting section. Although very few firms have the bichromatic electronic sorter shown here on the right. the unit is very effective for sorting out both unripe and fermented beans which are often overlooked previously because of less sophisticated sorting procedures (monochromatic equipment).

succession of processes the best known of which are roasting and packaging.

But there are two other important and necessary operations: sorting and blending. The former is necessary in case there are imperfect beans in the consignment, an eventuality that has become more frequent because of less thorough processing and the practice of stripping. As we have already seen, the berries and beans are repeatedly sorted during the wet process; even so it is possible for slightly fermented and unpleasant-smelling beans to be present in washed coffees, and these can be eliminated through electronic sorting using ultraviolet rays. In coffees processed by the dry method, on the other hand, because less care is taken at harvesting, unripe or over-ripe berries are often found, which can be removed through bichromatic electronic sorting which uses the information contained in the colour of the silver-skin of the bean to judge whether the bean is at the proper stage of ripeness. Unfortunately, such sophisticated sorting machines are not always available in coffee producing countries, because they are very costly and very difficult to operate. Moreover there are relatively few imperfect beans, let us say one in a thousand, so the producer does not consider it necessary to remove them.

But the roaster may think differently, since just one rotten bean, if it winds up in a cup of coffee, can spoil both the taste and the aroma. In fact there are some substances present in defective beans that are detectable even when greatly diluted: this is the case with substances that derive from the processes of fermentation that have affected berries known as stinkers, and with trichloroanisole, a chemical substance that gives coffee the so-called "Rio-smell", and wine the so-called "cork-smell". Trichloroanisole is noticeable even when there is only one part per 100 milliards. This is why the use of electronic sorting is slowly spreading among coffee-roasting firms

The samples analyzed by a roasting firm – especially those from lots pending sales closure – are kept in its "sample classification" section. When the lot arrives, the filed sample is taken out and a comparison is made to see if the sample's characteristics correctly match those of the lot. Any contestations are resolved by an appropriate board of experts who rule if the roasting firm is entitled to reimbursement for damages and establish the relative amount to be paid to the firm.

which pride themselves on the quality of their product.

Sorting can also be done on the roasting machine, using sorting machines similar to those already mentioned: but in this case it is more of a "cosmetic" operation for the purpose of removing beans that are over-roasted, but not necessarily defective and affected by almost no organoleptic deterioration.

Blending, on the other hand, basically serves two purposes: to enhance the quality of the coffee and maintain a consistently high standard. As a rule every consignment contains coffee of predominantly one type of taste (for example mild or bitter) and one particular aroma. Blending makes it possible to obtain a balance between the different flavour components (bitter, sour, sweet) and a strong aroma that has a wide spectrum of characteristics.

The particular characteristic aroma of any one coffee should not predominate, but combine with the others to give a richer blend.

A further consideration, as with all natural produce, is that from time to time and from year to year the organoleptic properties of the coffee consignments may vary; it is only by adjusting the proportions of the different types of coffee that these variations can be remedied and a consistent blend produced.

Top: The "heart" of an electronic sorter. The raw beans stream in front of the photoelectric cells at a rate of 200 beans per second. When a bean's colour is not within the prescribed limits. an air jet eliminates it. *Above:* Berries at various stages of ripeness. Green berries have unripe beans. which are eliminated by the electronic bichromatic sorter. The sorter's photoelectric cells are sensitive to the shades of green and red light reflected from the beans dropping past them.

The "creation" of a blend of coffee is not unlike the blending of wines, typical of champagne production; the blending may be done before or after roasting, as in wine making either the grapes or the wines may be blended. Blending before roasting has the advantage of giving a greater homogeneity of taste and aroma and makes it possible to carry out quality controls subsequently on the roasted coffee; the disadvantages are that it is more difficult to obtain an even result when roasting beans from different consignments, as these will probably be of different size and weight. The problem does not arise if blending is done after roasting, given that each lot of beans is roasted separately; but in this case the taste and the aroma of the product are less consistent and less well blended, and quality controls on the blend are not productive, given that the beans come from different roastings, so if there is something wrong it is impossible to know which of these is responsible.

Roasting

Green coffee, after the processing it has undergone in the producing countries, will keep several years without any significant deterioration in quality. Before it can be

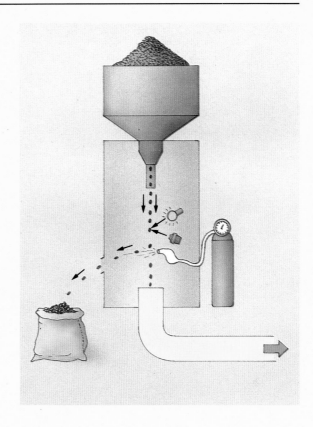

used, however, it still has to go through another very important process: roasting, through which it will develop its characteristic aroma.

Once roasted, however, coffee will not keep for so long, and without sophisticated packaging, for only a few months. For this reason coffee is normally roasted in the consumer country, to reduce the inter-

The picture schematically shows how the electronic sorter works. The beans dropping down from a hopper are illuminated by a light source (white or ultraviolet, depending on the type of machine). The light reflected by each bean is picked up by one or more photoelectric cells located in the immediate vicinity of the dropping beans. The signals received by the cells go to an electronic processing unit which analyzes the signals and decides whether or not the bean should be rejected. Reject beans are blown out of the bean stream by an air jet. There are two types of electronic sorting machines, monochromatic and bichromatic. The former analyzes the total amount of white light reflected off each bean, while the latter analyzes just the green and red light frequencies.

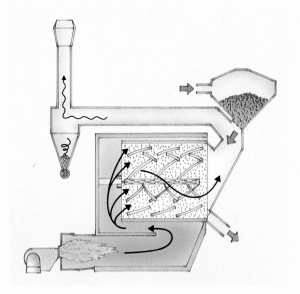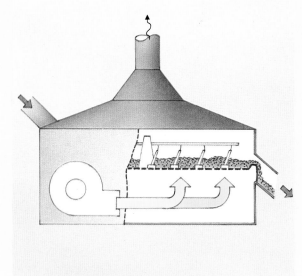

val between roasting and consumption. Coffee-roasting is a process of pyrolysis which, by increasing the temperature of the coffee from room temperature to 200-230 degrees ideally within the space of 10-15 minutes (in theory roasting can take a few minutes or half an hour), brings about marked physical and chemical changes in the beans that improve the quality of coffee and make it easier to prepare.

The main physical changes are loss of weight (from 15 to 20 per cent) due chiefly to water evaporation and the release of certain heavy gases such as car-bon dioxide, which, reaching very high pressures within the cells (20-25 atmospheres), cause the bean to swell, increasing its volume by about 60 per cent.

Loss of weight and increase of volume are accompanied by a change in the structure of the bean, which becomes less elastic and more brittle (which makes it easier to grind). Its colour changes from green to brown through the caramelising of the sugar and other carbohydrates and the formation of certain pigmented substances produced by chemical reactions known as Strecker's reactions.

These take place only at the highest

Top left: Discontinuous-cycle, drum-type roaster. The hot air from the blower (*bottom*) passes through the drum containing the raw beans. In about 10 or 15 minutes, the roasting temperature of 200-230 °C is reached. Once roasted, the beans are unloaded into the cooling hopper (*top right*) where the beans are stirred mechanically while cool air is sent through them. Water is often sprayed into the cooling air.

temperatures, so the higher the temperature the darker the coffee, whereas the coffee remains "light" if roasting is stopped at around 200 degrees.

The main chemical changes however concern the presence of some groups of substances that vary before and after roasting, and the formation of new compounds. Thus we see the water content drop from about 10 per cent to less than 1 per cent, fatty substances increase from 12 to 16 per cent, sugars drop from 10 to 2 per cent and chlorogenic acids drop from 7 to 4.5 per cent. Trigonelline also falls from 1 to 0.5 per cent, while the nitrogenous substances go up from 12 to 14 per cent; the caffeine, cellulose, pectin and ashes remain virtually unchanged

This roasting facility has two drum-type roasting machines. All the relative controls are automated, as can be seen in the centre of the photo. However, a roasting expert always has to be on hand to supervise the operations, set up the various programmes, and check all the graphs at regular intervals to detect any abnormal condition requiring his immediate intervention.

Above: Freshly-roasted beans being cooled in the cooling hopper. The beans are mechanically stirred while cool air is passed through them. *Left:* A close view of the shiny beans. When water is used, the resulting steam (the temperature of the steam exceeds 200 °C) dilates the pores of the cells, which helps release the gases and volatile aromas produced during roasting.

however. The new substances that develop derive from the pyrolytic process and after roasting represent about 30 per cent of the weight of the bean: these are caramel, carbon dioxide and about 700 substances that compose the volatile aromas. These are formed by the so-called Maillard's reactions (from the name of the man who discovered them), which begin at about 160 degrees and continue until roasting is stopped. Along with the aromatic substances inside the cell carbon dioxide develops, causing it to swell up to the point that many explode if the temperature becomes excessive (let us say 230 degrees).

The explosion of a limited number of cells causes rather strange popping sounds at two moments during roasting when the

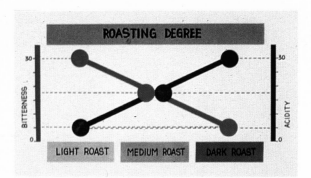

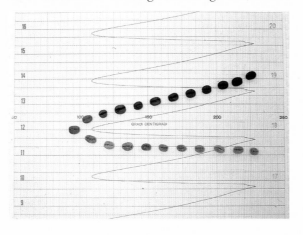

coffee is thus said to be "squeaking".

When the cell wall splits through too much pressure, gas is released as well as volatile aromas; this explains why, when increasing the final temperature of the roast, up to a certain point the aromas increase and then diminish. Not only does the quantity of aroma vary in accordance with the temperature but also the corresponding degrees of bitter and acid taste: bitterness increases with the temperature whereas acidity diminishes. So the more lightly roasted coffees have an acidulous taste, while the darker roasts on the contrary are more bitter.

The most delicate stage in the roasting process is the final stage; above 200 degrees the chemical reactions, hitherto endothermic (heat absorbing) become exothermic (heat producing). The increase in temperature of the coffee therefore

Top: The diagramme shows that the higher the roasting temperature, the more bitter the final drink, although higher roasting temperature reduces final acidity.
Above: The colour of the bean changes according to the temperature of the roasting machine. When the raw bean is first introduced into the machine, the temperature drops and then gradually increases until it exceeds 225 °C. During this interval, the colour of the bean – which is initially green – goes to yellow, then to light brown and finally to dark brown. *Right:* The higher the temperature, the darker the bean becomes.

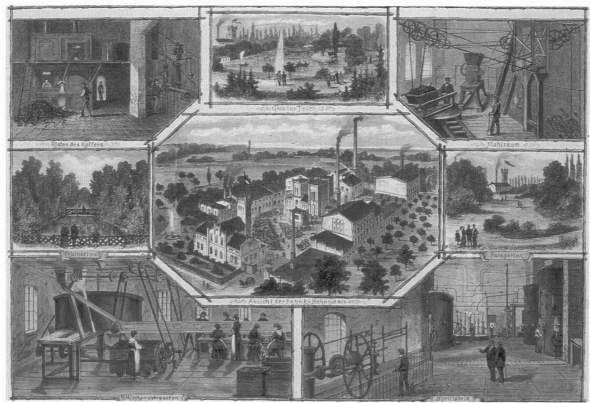

becomes more rapid because in addition to the heat applied by the roaster (which must be reduced) there is the heat released by the chemical reactions. Roasting can be stopped automatically by a temperature gauge or else manually by testing the roasting coffee to check on its colour: once the desired colour is reached, the roast is tipped into the cooling hopper.

Here the beans are continually kept moving in a flow of cold air which is often also sprayed with water. The use of water in the cooling process, although it speeds it up, is damaging to the quality of the coffee in at least three ways: it increases its weight reducing its yield, it accelerates the loss of carbon dioxide and volatile aromas and lastly it increases the chemi-

This old German print shows an overall view of a coffee-bean roasting establishment and detail views of the various sections: roasting (using wood and coal!), grinding, mixing, and packaging. All modern bean-roasting firms today have these same basic processing phases.

cal instability (water is a catalyst) of the blend, accelerating its degenerative processes.

The most common coffee-roasting machines work in discontinuous cycles: in the course of one cycle they roast a batch of green beans.

As it is heated the coffee may be blended in two ways: with the use of a rotating drum, the interior and walls of which are lapped by the flow of superheated air, or else by creating such an intense "cyclone" of hot air that it keeps the beans aloft, tossing about in the vortices.

Machines of this latter type give a better exchange of heat between the air and the coffee, making possible the "rapid roast" or "high yield" that may only take 60 seconds.

Such short roasting times enable the producer to increase the capacity of his equipment and reduce the weight loss, but do not allow the coffee to develop — through Maillard's reactions — its volatile aromas, nor do they reduce the percentage of trigonelline and chlorogenic acids which will be noticeable in the coffee, giving it a bitter or unpleasant taste and making it less digestible.

Both the traditional rotating drum machines and the more modern machines have a device for sucking out the silver skins that, not being elastic, are shed when the beans swell.

Packaging

After roasting the coffee is ready for consumption, but this generally happens at different times and in different places, hence the problem of how to transport the coffee and keep it fresh. In fact if it is left exposed to the air, roasted coffee loses its freshness and aroma within a couple of weeks: carbon dioxide is released from the beans, taking with it the volatile aromas, while the humidity and oxygen in the air "finish the job" by triggering or accelerating the processes of oxidization. Oxidization cannot occur at once because the carbon dioxide contained at high pressure in the cells acts as an anti-oxidant; once it has been released it no longer performs this important function. So packaging is designed to facilitate the transport and prolong the shelf-life of the coffee. Some forms of packaging answer only the former purpose: packets or tins that allow gases to enter or escape freely, because there is no kind of "seal". To keep coffee fresh for longer, more sophisticated forms of packaging must be used, and these fall into three groups.

Below: Roasted coffee-bean cells. The beans on the left have been preserved in the normal manner, while the ones on the right have been pressurized. In contrast with what happens in the former case, the oils inside the cells in the latter case are forced out. This oil (seen in white) surrounds the cells and prevents the volatile aromas contained inside the cells from escaping. Although both of the bean samples shown were roasted on the same day, the beans preserved under pressure have higher quality and more aroma.

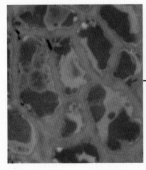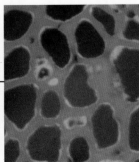

The first is vacuum packing: the packets or tins are filled with coffee, any air is expelled and then they are hermetically sealed. Carbon dioxide and a good part of the volatile aromas are expelled together with the air, but at least the air outside can no longer reach the contents. With this method, much used for ground coffee, the contents will keep well for over three months.

The second method entails the use of containers with a small one-way valve, that allows the gases released by the coffee to escape, but prevents any air from entering. Before sealing the containers, already filled with coffee, a vacuum may also be created or even better a vacuum combined with a combination of inert gases (carbon dioxide and nitrogen). Even without these additional measures, coffee packed in this way, generally ground coffee, will keep for more than a year. In fact the air initially inside the container is progressively expelled by the gases produced by the coffee (every kilo produces from 15 to 20 litres) and so no longer poses any threat to the contents. A comparison between this method and vacuum packing clearly shows that less aroma is lost initially with the former.

The third method is compression: the coffee is packed under inert gas pressure. Above all this requires airtight, strong containers, generally of metal; the coffee is vacuum-packed, the air removed and replaced with inert gases at low pressure and the containers are hermetically sealed. A safety valve prevents any excess pressure that may be caused by the gases produced by the coffee sealed in the container.

With this method the beans remain under gas pressure all the time, which has two main advantages: firstly shelf-life, which may be longer than three years because the coffee cells always contain carbon dioxide, a "natural" anti-oxidant, and because there can be no air in the container; hence the preservation of the volatile aromas, which in time tend to become "fixed" to the fatty substances that coat the cell wall. This factor is of particular interest to anyone making espresso coffee, because it is only by this method that the fats can be emulsified, conferring a wealth of aromas to the cup of coffee.

As we have seen, coffee blends may be made with beans or ground coffee: "connoisseurs" generally prefer to use beans, not only for their appearance but because they retain their taste and aroma for longer.

Preceding pages: How people used to have coffee at home. A long time ago, beans would be roasted and ground at home by the consumers themselves. *Below:* How coffee was packaged in the '30s. The packages were pressurized. Francesco Illy got the original idea of packaging the beans under inert-gas pressure. Pressurized packaging was ideally suited for coffee used making "espresso", because the espresso machine's high water pressure could emulsify the aromatic oils preserved by the gas-pressure packaging and transfer them directly to the final drink in the coffee cup. *Right:* An excerpt from an old French encyclopedia showing the entire coffee cycle from the plant to the cup.

Le Caféier est un bel arbrisseau toujours vert. Ses feuilles ressemblent à celles du laurier : il produit des fruits rouges semblables à des cerises, et contenant deux noyaux qui sont les grains de Café. Ses fleurs ressemblent à celle du jasmin blanc et ont une odeur délicieuse.

Le Caféier pousse à Java, aux Indes, au Brésil, aux Antilles, etc. Le même arbre portant à la fois fleurs et fruits, la récolte se fait pour ainsi dire de manière continue, mais surtout en mai. Des nattes sont étendues sous les arbres qu'on secoue pour faire tomber les fruits mûrs.

Les fruits sont portés sous des meules qui écrasent la pulpe dont les noyaux ou grains de Café sont entourés. Les grains sont alors mis dans des sacs et chargés sur les navires à destination d'Europe. Le Café compose ainsi le chargement d'une quantité de navires du plus fort tonnage.

Le Café est débarqué dans les ports de mer d'Europe, dont voici les cinq plus grands marchés : Le Hâvre, Londres, Amsterdam, Anvers et Hambourg. De là, les chemins de fer répandent la précieuse denrée sur le continent dans toutes les directions.

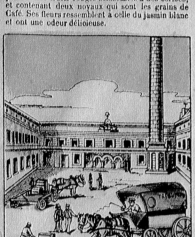

Le Café arrive alors chez les marchands en gros : une quantité considérable des Cafés des meilleures plantations est expédiée directement à l'usine **Trébucien**, 25 avenue de Vincennes, à Paris, dans laquelle on prépare le célèbre **Café des Gourmets** que le monde entier connaît.

Là, dans d'immenses magasins où les Cafés sont entassés, on procède au mélange des différentes sortes pour unir la force des unes au goût délicat des autres. Ce mélange fait dans des proportions longtemps étudiées permet d'utiliser les qualités spéciales des Cafés de chaque provenance.

Le Café mélangé est versé dans des trémies d'où il tombe dans les appareils à *torréfaction* par des conduites en tôle qui mesurent mécaniquement la quantité nécessaire pour chaque brûloir mû à la vapeur et tournant régulièrement dans de grands fourneaux où les grains de Café sont uniformément torréfiés.

Pour éviter l'évaporation de leur arôme, les grains de Café sont *enrobés* d'une couche mince mais continue de sucre caramélisé par la vapeur, puis refroidis brusquement sur de longues tables métalliques : Cet *enrobage* et ce brusque refroidissement empêchent toute évaporation. Le Café passe alors aux moulins qui le réduisent en poudre.

Le Café moulu arrive immédiatement aux ouvrières qui le pèsent exactement et en remplissent des boîtes de fer blanc contenant 250 ou 500 grammes. Dans ces boîtes hermétiques, le Café conserve indéfiniment son arôme. Puis, d'autres ouvrières collent les Étiquettes sur les boîtes et les portent au Magasin.

On emballe alors le **Café des Gourmets** dans des caisses destinées à tous les pays du Monde, même aux pays qui l'ont produit : car le **Café des Gourmets** est connu partout; la torréfaction spéciale du Café par les procédés de la Maison **Trébucien** est une industrie absolument française dont l'équivalent n'existe nulle part.

Des camions portent enfin le **Café des Gourmets** à toutes les gares pendant que des voitures plus légères portent chaque jour aux Épiciers de Paris et des environs les quantités dont ils ont besoin. Chaque jour, plus de 4000 kil. de **Café des Gourmets** se répandent ainsi dans toute la France.

Chez tous les épiciers, les acheteurs qui en ont une fois goûté, ne veulent plus que du **Café des Gourmets** et, depuis 25 ans, la qualité reste invariable. Ils ont bien soin de s'assurer que c'est du véritable **Café des Gourmets** qu'on leur donne, car les contrefacteurs sont nombreux et, quoique toujours condamnés, ils ne se découragent pas.

FALSIFICATIONS DU CAFÉ

Chicorée, Carottes torréfiées, Glands de chêne, Orge & Avoine grillées, Foie de Cheval, Noir animal épuisé, Briques pilées, Vieux-Marcs, Terre-Glaise, &ª

Le public doit enfin apprendre ce que certains fabricants peu scrupuleux lui vendent comme du Café : la santé publique y est intéressée, et il faut une bonne fois que l'on sache quelles drogues abominables certaines concurrences osent vendre vis-à-vis du **Café des Gourmets** qui, lui,...

Aussi boit-on trop souvent, hélas ! à la place de Café des décoctions atroces qui n'en contiennent guère ! Le goût détestable et les propriétés malfaisantes de ces drogues malpropres pourraient être évités par les consommateurs si, au lieu d'acheter leur Café au hasard, ils prenaient...

Afin que le public soit bien et dûment édifié, voici la boîte du **Café des Gourmets** telle que le public doit l'acheter et l'exiger. Ces boîtes ainsi scellées au nom de la maison **Trébucien** ne contiennent que des Cafés de choix torréfiés dans les meilleures conditions, avec l'enrobage préservatif et conservateur de l'arôme indiqué sur les Éti...

TRÉBUCIEN
CAFÉ DES GOURMETS
ARÔME CONCENTRÉ
ÉCONOMIE & FORCE
PRIX DE LA BOITE 1.65

Aussi les consommateurs du **Café des Gourmets** sont-ils de plus en plus nombreux et ils lui trouvent toujours le goût exquis et le parfum agréable qui ont fait sa réputation. La production de l'usine **Trébucien** augmente sans cesse et elle représente déjà à elle seule plus de la moitié partie de la consommation totale du Café en France.

MANKIND
· AND ·
COFFEE

The last three centuries bear witness to an ever closer, today almost indissoluble link between mankind and coffee. If we go further back in time, indeed to millions of years ago, we find that this link has much more ancient origins. In fact it is hard to tell which first appeared on Earth, the coffee plant or man; some claim that coffee came first. From the geographical point of view too, the origins of man and coffee show a surprising closeness. The earliest remains of *homo sapiens* were found in central East Africa: the first coffee plants were discovered not far away, in Kaffa in South-West Ethiopia. Here coffee plants grew wild, as they still do today in other countries of Central Africa.

Although their origins in time and place are so close, the paths of mankind and coffee were only to cross in relatively recent times, although not so recent for the discovery of coffee to be precisely datable. Indeed there are several legends relating to its discovery, two of which are the best known. The first tells how the goatherd Kaldi, grazing his flock on the upland plains of Ethiopia, noticed that his goats would become particularly frisky after eating the leaves and berries of a particular shrub. He decided to try some himself, and thus discovered the invigorating and exhilarating effects of coffee. So he took the "magic" berries to a nearby monastery where the abbot, believing them to be the work of the Devil, threw them into the fire. This released the aroma of the coffee, so the berries were hastily rescued from the flames and the monks learned how to make the hot black beverage we know today. The monks considered coffee to be a gift from God as it helped them to stay awake during prayers. The second legend has even more direct divine connotations: it tells how the Archangel Gabriel came to the aid of Mohammed, who was about to be overcome by sleep, by bringing him some coffee from heaven. After a few sips Mohammed felt so invigorated that he was able to "unhorse forty men and make forty women happy". Regardless of such charming legends we know that for a long period coffee was used in a very different way from the beverage to which we are accustomed. Initially the berries were eaten whole, then the seeds or beans were extracted, ground and mixed with animal fat to make them easier to eat when travelling. It was, it seems, only after the year 1000 A.D. when the Arabs discovered how to boil water, that they first made coffee as an infusion, initially using the green beans and subsequently learning to roast and grind them before boiling them in water.

The name "coffee" does not derive, as might be thought, from Kaffa (its place of origin)

Facing title: A young Arab woman sips her coffee. The drinking of coffee is considered a ritual in many countries. *Right:* In Algeria, the ritual is performed both outdoors and indoors, the latter in coffee-houses which are not too different from the *qahveh khaneh,* the original Constantinople coffee-house of long ago.

 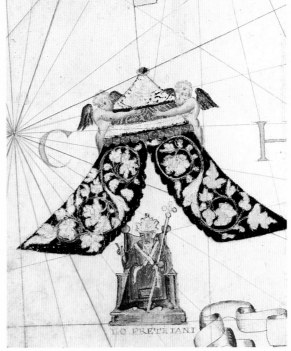

but from the Arab word *qahwa* meaning wine, coffee or any drink made from plants. Indeed, when coffee reached Europe, at the beginning of the 17th century, it was often called "the wine of Arabia". It is said that the first real quantity of coffee reached the Western world through the Turks, who left several sacks of coffee behind after their defeat at the gates of Vienna in 1683. The Austrians quickly learned to roast it and make the aromatic beverage which they served with cakes – called *kipfel* – shaped like crescent moons in celebration of the defeat of the Turks. Others say that coffee was first imported into Europe by Venetian merchants from 1615 onwards. What is certain is that the end of the 17th century saw the opening of the first coffee-houses to serve the new beverage, which was rapidly to become popular throughout Europe and the United States. Whilst the coffee plant is believed to have originated in the upland plains of Ethiopia,

Above left: The Sultan of Turkey – known as the "Great Turk". *Above right:* "Lo Prete Iani" (John the Priest). Ethiopia's legendary king. Both are shown on 16th century navigation charts. probably the same ones used by the sailors aboard the coffee merchant ships that travelled the Mocha-Venice route.

the beverage itself was first introduced and developed by the Arabs. Whereas the inhabitants of those areas where coffee plants grew wild would eat the green beans, possibly grinding them, it was the Arabs who began to turn the coffee into a beverage. Initially they procured the raw material from its land of origin, but by the 14th century they had already started to cultivate plants, taken during their raids, in the area of Yemen. Some believe that the plants may have reached Yemen in the 13th century, in the course of the Abyssinian invasion of Arabia. But the Arabs were probably already familiar with coffee as a beverage by the end of the 10th century, or maybe even earlier. Initially the beverage was made by soaking the green beans for a long time in cold water; then came the use of boiling water but it was only at the end of the 14th century that the Arabs discovered the process of roasting. They would then grind the roasted beans and boil the ground coffee in water; thus was invented the magnificent infusion which was to conquer the world in the course of the ensuing centuries. It was only after the discovery of roasting that coffee quickly became a popular beverage throughout the entire Islamic world and in areas under Arab control as a result of Arab invasion. Its popularity was favoured by the fact that alcoholic drinks are forbidden by the Koran. So coffee would be drunk both at home and in the *qahveh khaneh*, the forerunners of today's coffee-bars, which rapidly increased in number with the growing popularity of coffee. Here, as well as drinking coffee, people could listen to music, play games of chance, and discuss many matters. It was because of this intellectual activity, often perceived by the rulers as subversive, that the *qahveh khaneh* were on three occasions declared illegal and ordered to shut down. But the bans came to nothing as the popularity of coffee and the places where it was served was such that the people repeatedly ignored them. In family life too coffee played an important role: initially the women regarded it with suspicion, not because of its taste but because of its stimulating effect on their husbands. Similarly, the rulers thought that coffee had a destabilising effect on family life. But the women too very soon began to drink the black beverage, enjoying its many beneficial effects; it became so important that one of the causes allowed by law for marital separation was a husband's refusal to procure coffee for his wife. The use of coffee extended not only throughout the entire Arab territory but also to lands occupied during Arab invasion such as the Balkans, Spain, India, North Africa and Turkey.

An old picture showing a street vendor selling "Arabian wine", as coffee was first called in Europe. This typically Arabic custom was also exported to Europe – especially to Paris and other French cities – before the "invention" of the French café near the end of the 18th century.

To satisfy the growing demand, coffee-growing in the region of Yemen became more and more extensive and the Arabs tried every way they could to retain their monopoly of coffee production. In this they succeeded only for a short time because fertile seeds, easily concealed despite stringent controls, were very soon carried to neighbouring countries to start new plantations. And so, from Arabia the "cradle of coffee", both consumption and production of the coffee began steadily to spread, destined in time to reach far-distant peoples and places.

Coffee was known only by repute in European countries in the 16th century. Many travellers would talk of the exotic beverage

Preceding pages: The siege of Vienna during the war of 1683-1699. This painting by Frans Geffels – which dates from that period – is on view in the Historical Museum of Vienna. The wonderful new coffee drink was introduced to the Viennese by the Turks. *Above:* An old picture showing a few of the basic phases of coffee's long trip from the producer to the consumer.

on their return from the Orient. The best known accounts are by Prospero Alpino who describes the coffee plant in his book *De Plantis Aegypti*, 1592, and by Pietro della Valle. This famous man of letters had occasion to observe and subsequently describe the custom of coffee drinking already widespread in the Orient. This was at the beginning of the 17th century but the green beans had still not reached the Western world. Historians generally agree on 1615 as the date of the first importation of coffee into Europe by the Venetians. The decline of the economic power of Venice had already begun in the 16th century, due to the Portuguese who established their supremacy in the spice trade and the English and the Dutch who, albeit calling at Venice, were competing with the Venetian ships and merchants. In an attempt to regain lost ground the Venetians exploited their good relations with the Arabs, who still held the monopoly of coffee production, and began a new and profitable trade. The green beans were loaded in the

Coffee plants used to grow wild in the Abyssinian highlands. The Arabs invented the coffee drink, which was first made by mixing the beans with fatty substances and then boiling the mixture in water to make a brew. However, the aromatic drink as we know it today got its start at the end of the 14th century when the Arabs learned to roast the beans.

port of Mocha and, once unloaded in Venice, they would be distributed to the pharmacies and used for medicinal purposes: in fact coffee was initially known for its various therapeutic properties. But very soon, apparently as early as 1624, the Venetians learned to roast the beans and prepare the aromatic beverage. Its popularity was fostered by the Botteghe del Caffè, which first appeared in 1647 (some say 1683) and were initially called "Botteghe delle Acque e dei Ghiacci" because they served drinks made with water and ice. Whilst the black beverage was becoming increasingly popular in Venice both in the coffee-shops and at home, there was also a growing demand for coffee in other European countries. Venice thus became the source of supply of the raw material to neighbouring countries, especially the Germanic people. The "Fondaco dei Tedeschi", still in existence near the Rialto Bridge, was where the coffee from Arabia would be unloaded, stored and possibly roasted before passing into foreign hands. Meanwhile in Venice the early coffee-shops had evolved into more refined and sophisticated establishments, offering a greater range of refreshments and "services". The first of these was opened in 1720 by Floriano Francesconi and called "Caffè della Venezia Trionfante", notwithstanding the difficult military and economic situation of the time. The original name – perhaps chosen from the desire to encourage or flatter the rulers – in time changed to "Caffè Florian", after the name of the founder: as well as coffee, other drinks and sweetmeats were served. Various newspapers and reviews were also available and soon Florian's became a centre of cultural and commercial exchange. Its success was such that within a few years the number of cafés on St. Mark's Square had reached thirty: Florian's main rival was, and today still is, the "Caffè Quadri", which faced it on the opposite side of the square and was opened only a few years after Florian's. The popularity of these coffee-houses in Venice became so great that in 1759 they numbered 206. Thanks to Carlo Goldoni, who in 1750 wrote his comedy *La bottega del caffè*, we can still savour the atmosphere of those Venetian establishments, forerunners of today's coffee bars and cafés. The Venetians are to be credited with having been the first to import coffee from Arabia and introduce it into Europe. For almost a century, up to the early 18th century, they tried to hold on to their monopoly of the coffee trade. The Dutch on the other hand are to be credited with having started coffee production outside the Arab countries, which until the 17th century had retained their monopoly, even roasting or

"Trip Through Happy Arabia" – written by a Frenchman in 1716 – describes an expedition that left the port of Mocha for the court of the King of Yemen. one of the countries where coffee plants were first cultivated. Naturally. the book also relates the history of the origin and development of this new drink that also became very popular in France.

boiling the beans before selling them to foreigners, to prevent them from sprouting in other lands. The Arab monopoly had already been cracked through a pilgrim, Baba Budan, who at the beginning of the 17th century had managed to smuggle seven fertile seeds to Mecca and thence to India, in the region of Mysore, where he had started new plantations. Perhaps as early as 1616, although more probably in 1690, some Dutchmen

Besides being the title of a famous play by Goldoni. "The Coffee-Shop" is also the title of this unsigned painting which belongs to the Banca Cattolica del Veneto collection, on view in Vicenza. The first Venetian coffee-shops were called "Botteghe delle Acque e dei Ghiacci", because this is where people could also get iced drinks. But the growing popularity of coffee changed the name to "Bottega del caffè" and, with more popularity, the name was shortened still further to "Caffè".

managed to get hold of some small coffee plants which were then very carefully cultivated in the greenhouses of the botanic gardens in Amsterdam. From here several plants were sent out to the Dutch colonies in the East Indies and in 1699 experimental coffee growing began in Java and Sumatra. The plants took root and grew well in the favourable climate. Within a few years the Dutch colonies had become the main suppliers of the coffee to Europe, due mainly to the enterprise of the Dutch East India Company, and Amsterdam became the main commercial centre for the coffee trade. The price of the green beans was fixed by the Dutch dealers, who did not hesitate to destroy part of the harvest if, through being too plentiful, it threatened to bring prices down. As well as being producers and traders, the Dutch also quickly became coffee consumers despite the prior popularity of tea. Both beverages had their partisans and to settle the argument King Gustav III of Sweden ordered a doctor to conduct an experiment with two twins. One was to drink only coffee, the other tea, to establish which of the two beverages had harmful effects on the health. The doctor died, the king died and at the venerable old age of 83 so did the twin who had drunk tea, so the contest came to an end and both beverages were absolved. The Dutch, unlike the Venetians, did not create special establishments for the drinking of coffee; they preferred to drink it at home, to the benefit of family relationships, rather than in coffee-houses that fostered new relationships, as occurred in the Venetian cafés. In any case coffee quickly came to play an important role in the economy and customs of the Dutch people. Albeit proud of their colonial coffee production and their commercial supremacy, they did not seek to retain a European monopoly. So much so that in 1714 the burgomaster of Amsterdam made a gift of a coffee plant to King Louis XIV of France. The French monarch had for some time been familiar with the virtues of coffee, which was habitually drunk at court: it is said that the innovation of adding sugar to the beverage is owed to one of his courtesans. Coffee was also appreciated by the French people, and this had brought about a huge increase in price. The plants given to the King of France were nursed in the greenhouses of Versailles, whence they were destined to set out on a great new adventure. In 1723 a captain Gabriel de Clieu, serving in the French colonies in Martinique, while on leave in the mother country asked if he could take a few small coffee plants back with him. Thus began the journey of coffee to the Americas, where it was to be cultivated more

The first *qahveh khaneh* made its appearance in Constantinople in the 16th century. Men went there to pass a pleasant hour or so, discuss business, listen to music and dissertations, and so on. Right from the start, therefore, coffee-houses or shops have been closely linked to culture. Some local "historic" cafés have survived for centuries and are still going strong.

extensively than in any other continent. The spread of coffee in the Americas may be described as an adventure in name and in deed. It is said that captain de Clieu had to overcome a thousand difficulties and make a thousand detours before he was able to realise his project of transplanting in Martinique a number of young plants brought from the greenhouses of Versailles. The year was 1723; the poor plants, loaded aboard a sailing ship, had to endure storms, calms, water rationing and even one passenger's attempts to damage them. Fortunately de Clieu kept a close watch over them, and paid them such attention and care, eventually even sharing his own water ration with them, that they reached Martinique. They were immediately transplanted and within a few years were

This old painting on view in the Jacobs-Suchard Museum in Zurich shows the typical activity that went on in early cafés. Today's "Turkish coffee" is made in exactly the same way as it was by the Turks years and years ago. On the right we see a man pouring "Turkish coffee" from the traditional *ibrik*.

growing strongly and being propagated, so that by 1777 it was calculated that there were already 18-19 million plants on the island, yielding enough coffee to satisfy three quarters of the demand in Europe. During the same period other European colonial powers were starting to grow coffee in their own colonies: the Spaniards in the West Indies and the English, who were the last to believe in the success of these new plantations, in Jamaica in 1730 and in India in 1740. From the island of Martinique the new crop quickly multiplied on the mainland too, in Guyana, which for a short time was under French dominion. Those who obtained new plants tried to keep them to themselves, to avoid the growing risk of competition. It was through his personal charm that a Portuguese gentleman, a certain Francisco de Melo Palheta, succeeded in procuring some plants and taking them to Brazil to start what were to become the largest plantations in the world. It is said that he beguiled the wife of the governor of Guyana, who sent him some coffee plants skillfully disguised in a gift of flowers on the occasion of his visit to a neighbouring country in 1727. This romantic story is another of the legends surrounding coffee; the date is in fact questionable, and to this day there is disagreement in Brazil as to the date when the plantations originated: was it 1726 (prior to Palheta's romantic adventure) or 1735? Historians still cannot agree. One thing is certain: in Brazil the plants found ideal soil and climate. The country was destined to become the world's leading coffee producer, and coffee would be its chief source of wealth. The name of Brazil's best-known coffee, Santos, derives from that of Alberto Santos-Dumont, who in his turn had attached his mother's maiden name to his own. Alberto was the son of Henriquens, one of the first

pioneers of flight, and he was called the "Coffee King", having managed to plant 5 million coffee plants on his land. In the following years coffee-growing spread to other countries of South and Central America: to Mexico in 1740, to Venezuela in 1784, and only at the end of the century to Colombia, now the second largest producer in the

Left: A plantation owner at the turn of the century oversees the harvesting of coffee berries. If not trimmed, the plants can grow to a height of about 10 metres. In any case, the natives still have to use ladders to reach the upper branches. *Above:* Gabriel de Clieu – who is credited with having brought the first coffee plants to the New World – watches over his precious cargo during the long crossing of the Atlantic.

world. As a consumer good, coffee had reached the New World even before de Clieu's young plants, but further North, in North America, more precisely in 1660 in New Amsterdam, which within four years was to be conquered by the English and renamed New York. The English found the custom of drinking coffee already well established, albeit still the prerogative of the more prosperous classes. The other social classes were still fond of tea, which was not however destined to prevail for long. In fact in 1773 King George imposed a heavy tax on tea: the people rebelled at once and the citizens of Boston even attacked the English ships and threw their cargo of tea into the sea. This episode has gone down in history as the "Boston Tea Party", and it marked a change in the fortunes of coffee in North America, where within a few years it became the national beverage, as it still is today.

Ever since coffee has been consumed in countries far from the countries that produce it, ships have been used for the transport of the raw material. Perhaps the earliest document describing the long journey of the green beans is the *Mercure Galant* of Paris which as early as 1696 mentioned Jeddah as the main port for shipping coffee beans cultivated in the area around Mecca. The second stage of the journey was Suez, where the beans would be unloaded and transported by camel as far as Alexandria, and there loaded onto the waiting Venetian and French ships. The former would then set sail for Venice, the latter for Marseilles. The

This etching by M. Th. Bray shows natives in Suriname (Dutch Guyana) carrying out "beneficiamento" operations. Most of these operations are done mechanically today, although it takes many manhours to produce a sack of colonial coffee (only a few kilogrammes are available from each plant).

first great coffee route was undoubtedly that of the Eastern Mediterranean, where Dutch and English ships followed in the wake of the Venetians and the French. At the beginning of the 18th century, when the Dutch established the first plantations in Java and Sumatra, the ships which followed the route from the Far East would add this valuable commodity to their cargoes. The new route was very much longer and more exacting than the former, entailing the circumnavigation of the entire continent of Africa and in particular the dangerous rounding of the Cape of Good Hope. During the same period new coffee routes opened from Central and then South America, allowing Europeans and subsequently North Americans to use beans produced in Martinique, Guyana, Brazil, Jamaica, Mexico and the other tropical countries of America which were converted to growing the "green gold". The shipping routes from the Far East were sailed mainly by the Dutch, English, Spanish and Portuguese ships, whereas the American routes were sailed by the French, English and Portuguese. In the course of the last three centuries the cultivation of coffee has extended to more than seventy countries, all situated between the Tropic of Cancer and the Tropic of Capricorn, where the climate suits the plants. Today, in addition to the old Mediterranean route and the routes from the Far East and Central and South America, there are the routes from East and West Africa, to transport the produce of Ethiopia, Kenya, Tanzania and Madagascar on the one side,

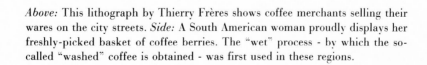

Above: This lithograph by Thierry Frères shows coffee merchants selling their wares on the city streets. *Side:* A South American woman proudly displays her freshly-picked basket of coffee berries. The "wet" process - by which the so-called "washed" coffee is obtained - was first used in these regions.

121

and of the Ivory Coast, Cameroon and Zaire on the other, to mention only the most important suppliers. Although the distances are as great as ever, progress has meant that they are covered in a much shorter time. Instead of the vulnerable sailing ships of the 18th century, we now have the powerful container-ships of today, which make it possible to bring the bags from America to Europe in under two weeks, as against the months required by sailing ships. Transport became more reliable with the introduction of motorships, which are not slowed by calms and come safely through storms.

The opening of the Suez Canal was also a great help in the transport of coffee, enabling

ships that followed the routes from the East and from East Africa to avoid sailing around Africa; they thus saved many days' sailing and huge costs. In recent times the actual mode of transporting coffee has also been changed, in order to reduce the costs which at one time amounted to proportionately more than the product itself. The traditional sacks made from vegetable fibres neatly stacked in the hold of a ship have thus been replaced by containers. These were initially filled with sacks, but now the green beans are mechanically loaded straight into the container and mechanically unloaded on arrival. Any possible harmful effects on green coffee transported by container have been obviated by the use of ventilated containers and by the short duration of the voyage. Complications regarding the use of full-containers, however, have still to be solved.

Top: Coffee, the national American drink, is an important part of this outdoor meal. The traditional coffee pot with its truncated-cone shape (seen here near the campfire) followed the old pioneers through the West. *Above:* A berry-harvesting scene of by-gone days. The baskets loaded with picked berries were taken to the areas where the berries were spread on the ground to dry under the sun. *Right:* Old photographs of production sites in Central and South America.

A beautiful 19th century villa in the state of Rio in Brazil, where "Rio" coffee is made. The taste of this particular type of coffee is too "medicinal" for western palates, but is very popular in the Balcans, and most Yugoslavians and Greeks prefer it.

Other views of the same villa. The interiors live up to one's expectations. *Next pages:* A painting by Joseph Vernier, showing the Port of Marseille. For years, this was the only French port where colonial coffee could be unloaded. The sacks of coffee were transported overland from this port to Paris and the other French cities.

North Carolina Glas
GALERIE
HILGER
und das Kunsthistorische Museum
präsentieren:
BEATRICE OST'
SCHWARZER DRAH
INTELLIGENC
NSTHANDLUNG JULIUS HUMMEL
CKERSTRASSE 14, A-1010 WIEN
ON 12. FEBRUAR BIS 30. APRIL 1988
FFNUNGSZEITEN MO-FR 15-18 UHR, SA 10-13 UHR
Wege
aus der
UMKLAMMERUNG
Naturphilosophie
Psychologie
THEATRE
Das Kind mit
dem Bade
DRACHEN
DRACHEN
DRACHENGASSE 2 THEATER
GALERIE RIEDER
Maximilianstr. 22 München
Telefon 29 45 17
GEORG EISLER
Zeichnungen für Bücher
Wiener Secession
1010 Wien, Friedrichstraße 12
8. April – 15. Mai 1988
Günter Grass
KAMMERTHEATER STOK
7 BIS 30. JA
FR 15-18, SA 1

THE
COFFEE
DRINKING
CULTURE

The coffee-houses
of Constantinople and Europe

Ever since the Arabs discovered the coffee-roasting process at the end of the 14th century and invented the black beverage we know today, coffee has "led a double life": private and public. Whilst the former was and is associated with friendship and family life at home, over the years the latter has become associated with a range of social and cultural recreations. The first two coffee-houses were opened in Constantinople in 1554 and were so successful that within a few years the city was full of them.

They were called *qahveh khaneh* but were often known as "schools of wisdom" because they were much frequented by the most cultured and well-educated men, scholars and men of letters, who would discourse on poetry or politics, stimulated by the aromatic beverage.

Men could also go to the coffee-house to listen to music, play chess or *mancalah*, a game similar to backgammon, rather than listen to the fables and legends narrated by the professional story-tellers.

But they could also simply have discussions or make friends with other customers, sometimes from far-off lands.

Important deals would often be concluded over a steaming cup of coffee. In short the coffee-houses of Constantinople, forerunners of the European cafés, seethed with activities that stimulated the economy, the social life, the cultural and political life of the city.

It was because of these political activities that the rulers, fearful that conspiracies were being hatched, on at least three occasions banned these public meeting places.

But it was to no avail: the edicts closing down the *qahveh khaneh* were disregarded by the entire population, by now accustomed to coffee drinking and stimulated by the various activities that were part of the ritual.

When the first coffee-houses were opened in Europe the following century, they were shaped on those of Constantinople. Initially some enterprising traders, often from the East, tried to promote coffee-drinking among the middle to lower social classes, mindful of the popularity of coffee in Arab countries. But they had no success and the travelling salesmen and modest establishments soon gave way to splendid cafés which attracted a more cultivated and well-to-do clientele.

So in Venice, where coffee had been available since 1645 in the "Botteghe delle

Facing title: A client in a German café enjoys his cup of percolated coffee. Culture also played an important role in German cafés, and the posters on the walls invited customers to visit the museums, art galleries and other cultural events.
Right: An old café in Rome. Pope Clement VIII was another avid Roman coffee-lover and even gave the drink his benediction by baptizing it with holy water.

N. Bacquet.

Acque e dei Ghiacci", the "Caffé alla Venezia Trionfante", better known as Florian's, was founded in 1720 by Floriano Francesconi.

In Vienna the first establishment to serve coffee, in 1687, was the "Blue Flask" tavern, opened by a Georg Kolschitsky. He had played a leading role in the liberation of Vienna from the besieging Turks and had been rewarded with 500 sacks of coffee abandoned by the enemy in their flight. Knowing the Arab custom, he quickly learned to roast and blend the coffee, which was served with cakes shaped like the crescent moon (in honour of the victory over the Turks): this was the

Above: Interior of a coffee-house in London. at the time of Queen Anne. The activities which took place there were not different from those of Venetian and Parisian cafés. *Side:* A *garçon du café.* as was called the waiter who served the aromatic beverage. *Right:* This painting by Francesco Guardi depicts a coffee-shop in St. Mark's Square in Venice. Customers are shown while admiring and criticizing paintings; artistic. cultural and musical events were commonly organised in these rooms.

start of the famous *kipfel*, as well as the very Middle-European custom of serving cakes and sweetmeats with coffee. In Paris the first important café (still in existence, like Florian's) was the "Procope", opened by a Sicilian gentleman named Procopio dei Coltelli at the end of the 18th century. Today the Procope is a restaurant where one can still breathe the magic atmosphere of the first cafés of Europe. In London too, notwithstanding the deep-rooted custom of tea-drinking, numerous coffee-houses were opened: the first was apparently opened in 1652 by a certain Pasqua Rosée.

What those great European coffee-houses of the 17th century had in common was the original spirit of the coffee-houses of Constantinople: drinking coffee was not an end in itself so much as the stimulus for other social and cultural activities. In the coffee-houses you would meet artists, men of letters and politics, you could read the leading reviews or draw up important contracts. On the other hand, what was lost was the mystical atmosphere of the early oriental coffee-houses with their music, stories and legends of a far-off world. For many years the economy, culture and politics of European countries were stimulated and spread in the coffee-houses.

Cultural circles, poets and newspapers. Over a cup of coffee: culture and politics from the Age of Reason onwards

The phenomenon of the cafés, which spread from the end of the 17th century and throughout the 18th, was a European event, as was the Enlightenment or "Age of Reason" as the English and the French call it. The new cultural movement can be placed between the English Revolution (1688) and the beginning of the French Revolution (1789). The spread of cafés in Europe thus coincided with the Age of Reason. It was not only a coincidence of time but also of place, since as we have seen, it was in the cafés that men discussed literature, science, economics and politics.

Perhaps it was no mere coincidence but reciprocal influences: the cafés gave the protagonists of the new cultural movement the opportunity and the pretext to exchange ideas and opinions and to encourage each other; coffee helped these intellectual activities, with its virtue as a stimulant as vaunted by the Italian scholar Pietro Verri in the first number of a magazine named after the beverage.

The beneficial influence of coffee on the mind must also have been well-known to Voltaire, one of the leaders of the Age of

Photograph of the beginning of the century showing a *garçon du café* at Salonika. On the tray, a nargileh, often associated with the rite of coffee consumption in old Arabian coffee-houses. In Greece as well as in Turkey coffee is traditionally prepared by boiling.

Reason in France, of whom it is said that he drank fifty cups a day. In short, coffee at that time was important not only in pleasing the palate of the neo-intellectuals but also in stimulating and fostering the new concept of individual liberty, which was intolerant of the unjustified powers exercised by the Church and the Monarchy. This role of fostering liberty and independence, while also acting as a socializing force, is also to be found in the colonies of the American West and has survived unaltered to this day: you only have to enter a bar in Italy to see it in operation.

The cultural activity that revolved around the first cafés of Europe spread and intensified throughout the 18th and 19th

Woodcut by Frank Kirchbach, 1890. It shows Goethe reciting a poem to his mother, sister, and some friends in the neighbourhood of Frankfurt. The guests have been offered a cup of coffee as usual, to add to the pleasure of verses.

centuries, in the form of cultural circles and literary salons: in Italy the most famous of these were those of Aragno in Rome, Michelangelo in Florence and Fiorio in Turin, but they were to be found in all the main cities of Italy and Europe.

The cultural and political life associated with the cafés led to the publication in Milan, from June 1764 to May 1766, of a periodical entitled "Il Caffè". The editor in chief was the already mentioned Pietro Verri, assisted by his brother Alessandro, by Cesare Beccaria and numerous other intellectuals, all belonging to the Accademia dei Pugni.

The name of the review was provocatively different from the pompous names of the academic reviews of the time; the articles purported to relate or discuss conversations that took place in the Milanese shop of a Greek café proprietor. In reality they dealt with cultural and above all political matters, such as the moral analysis of society, morality in commerce and "the spirit of Italian letters".

Notwithstanding man's enormous progress in the last three hundred years, accompanied or more probably fostered by the clarification of thought helped by coffee, the issues treated by Verri are still those of the present day, and coffee is still here to help us face up to them.

Cafés that have made history: Florian, Greco, Pedrocchi, for those who have a taste for the exclusive

Cafés spread throughout Europe from the Age of Reason onwards, and over the centuries many of them have retained their original splendour and activities: it is in Italy, the country where coffee is so popular, that the largest number of these "historic cafés" have survived.

In Rome there is the Greco and the Aragno, in Naples the Gambrinus, in Florence the Giubbe Rosse and the Gilli, in Venice the Florian and the Quadri, in Padua the Pedrocchi, in Trieste the Tommaseo and the San Marco, in Turin the Platti, the San Carlo, the Fiorio, the Baratti & Milano.

All bear witness to a bygone age and the role played by coffee and the café in promoting the social, economic and cultural progress of humanity. They all continue to play their part in restoring body and mind, as well as providing a meeting place for fostering new relations.

Some of them are also the scene of organised meetings and debates, or concerts that recall the old French custom of the *café chantant*.

The most legendary of all is doubtless Florian's, which is also the oldest (1720).

Right: Two pictures of contemporary life in coffee-houses. Reading papers is a common activity, but sometimes also concerts, painting exhibitions or meetings, as well as presentations of books or new publishing programmes are organised to keep to a sort of cultural "mission".

Top: Two pictures of the Middle-European type of café. *Above left:* The splendid Bauer Café in East Berlin. *Above right:* The long dining hall of the Hungaria Café in Budapest. In keeping with an old national tradition. Hungarians have always been the biggest coffee-drinkers.

It faces onto St. Mark's Square in Venice, under the arcade of the Procuratie Nuove; the interior is divided into a number of small rooms ("Chinese", "Greek", "dei Quadri", "del Senato"), one of which has recently been reopened to the public after extensive restoration.

The walls are decorated with frescoes, paintings (some by Carlini) and gold inlay; the small tables of wood and marble and the chairs are very well preserved. Casanova once sat here, and Parini, D'Annunzio, Goethe, Dickens, Proust and countless other famous people.

Various newspapers as well as several reviews were founded here from 1760 onwards, of which the most important is Gaspare Gozzi's "Gazzetta Veneta".

The Caffè Florian in Venice, which dates back to 1720, is one of Europe's oldest and best-preserved "historic" cafés. The small rooms are connected by a corridor and are well furnished with paintings, frescoes and tinted stucco-work. It is actually very difficult to say which room is the most beautiful. The interior decoration, the authenticity which has not been adversely affected by the various restoration interventions over the years, give the feeling that time has stopped for these rooms.

Today you can admire the splendid decoration of these small rooms while sipping your coffee, or in summer you can sit at tables outside in St. Mark's Square and enjoy the unique view of the surrounding palazzi and the cathedral.

The Caffè Greco was opened a few years after Florian in Rome, on the via Condotti, close by the Piazza di Spagna. The modest-looking façade conceals a large establishment broken up into a series of small rooms connected by rather narrow corridors: the largest room, reserved for important clients, is the "Sala Rossa". The walls of the Caffè Greco are also decorated with old paintings, by Vincenzo Giovannini among others, and statues and statuettes; there is also a library containing old books and documents.

The list of famous people who have frequented the Caffè Greco is a long one: as well as artists and men of letters, the café has welcomed men of the Church such as Leo XIII and heads of state such as Louis I of Bavaria, King Constantine of Greece, President Kennedy and President Mitterand.

A visit to the Caffè Greco, in the heart of Rome, is still likely to afford a surprise encounter with leading personalities in the entertainment world and in public life.

The Caffè Pedrocchi is "younger" than Florian and the Caffè Greco; it was opened in 1831 by Antonio Pedrocchi who had inherited from his father Francesco an old and modest coffee-shop. Thanks to the design of the Venetian architect Giuseppe Jappelli, the Pedrocchi is today regarded as the "temple" of coffee. The establishment has recently been completely restored, to give the marble that covers the floors and walls its old lustre.

Outside, stone lions watch over the customers who sit at the small tables in summer; inside, there is a main room on the ground floor, where you can drink

Left: An outside view of the Central Café in Vienna, expecially famous for its "personalized" chocolates. *Above:* The window of the Caffè Greco in Rome. This historic café dates from 1760 and is fairly well preserved. It serves hundreds of people every day, which is at least partially due to the fact that it is located in the center of town (on via Condotti).

your coffee standing at the carved marble bar.

Upstairs there are ten interconnecting rooms, each decorated in a different way, where you can sit and drink your coffee during the winter months.

Different architectural styles combine in a seemingly haphazard but always pleasing way: it is worth taking the time to visit all the rooms as well as look at the outside. Recently, to satisfy a rather heterogeneous clientele – citizens of Padua who work in the city centre, tourists and visitors who come to admire – the manager of the Pedrocchi has decided to install a bar to serve, at lower prices, customers who are in a hurry, reserving the luxury of the old rooms for their more leisurely and particular customers. It is a good example of the historic cafés keeping up with the times, able to meet the demands of today while retaining the style of the past, giving the customer the chance to choose whichever he prefers.

Old cafés sometimes actually contain a wealth of interesting artistic and historic treasures, such as paintings, etchings, portraits, posters, etc. The discerning visitor, who approaches these cafés somewhat as though they were museums, is bound to discover fascinating insights on past events involving our cultural roots.

Top left: One of the dining rooms in the Caffè Pedrocchi in downtown Padua. *Top right:* The Gran Caffè Gambrinus in Naples, which dates back to the last century. The fascist regime forced it to close in 1939, but it reopened shortly afterwards, after having given up the use of most of its floor space for other purposes. *Above left:* The sign outside the Caffè Florian in Venice. *Above right:* Inside the Caffè Greco in Rome.

Left: The windows of the elegant Schwarzenberg Café in Vienna. *Above:* The interior of what is probably the Austrian capital's most important coffee-house – the Central Café – is almost completely wainscotted in wood, which provides a comfortable, quiet, relaxing atmosphere that takes one back into the past.

THE
SECRETS
OF
COFFEE

The history of coffee as a beverage

Coffee drinking, today so popular, almost certainly began with the Arabs, who discovered that a tasty and aromatic beverage could be made from coffee beans and water. Up to the 10th century in fact, man used coffee as a foodstuff in those regions where the plants grew wild. Initially they very probably ate only the thin layer of sweet pulp that surrounds the seeds or beans, until the "magic" stimulant properties of the beans were discovered. After this the local people began to eat the beans, which they pounded to a paste and mixed with animal fats. It is not surprising that this food enjoyed only limited popularity: the green beans hardly have a pleasant and appealing flavour!

Later came the idea of soaking the beans in water for days to produce a drink. It was only after the year 1000 that the Arabs discovered how to boil water, and began to boil the green beans instead of merely soaking them. It saved time, but the beverage that resulted was no better.

It was not until the 14th century that the Arabs discovered how to roast the beans, thereby adding a pleasing flavour to the stimulant properties of the drink. The roasted beans were first boiled whole in water, but then came the idea of grinding the beans, probably in a mortar; this produced an infusion with more flavour and aroma, because the increased contact surface between water and coffee meant that more of the substances contained in the latter could dissolve in the former. It is a mystery why this method of making coffee, invented by the Arabs and the only known method for over four centuries, should be known as "Turkish" coffee.

Coffee is still made in this way in several countries, notably Turkey and Greece. A variation of this method is infusion, the same method as used in making tea; instead of boiling the ground coffee in the water, boiling water is poured over the ground coffee. It is only recently that two other methods of coffee-making have been invented: the percolation method and the "espresso" method. In both of these the coffee, instead of being left to infuse in the water or actually boiled in it, simply has water pass through it, extracting and taking with it the substances in the ground coffee. In the percolation method the water passes through simply at the speed dictated by gravity, whereas in the espresso method the water is forced through under pressure, so that it extracts a greater quantity of the substances contained in the coffee.

Facing title: This 1930's photograph shows a young woman inviting the observer in a charming way to taste a good cup of coffee. *Left:* Sacks of coffee beans being unloaded in the traditional manner, which is becoming more and more rare. Nowadays it is more cost-effective to ship by container. Beans have even recently been shipped in bulk form (not sacked) in what are called "full-containers".

From the invention of the first "Turkish" coffee to the invention of the espresso method, which dates from the 19th century, coffee has developed not only a variety of methods of preparation but also a range of "accessories".

The idea of adding sugar to coffee is said to have originated with the court ladies of Louis XIV. Honey is sometimes used instead of sugar, and we have also learned to add milk, cream, spirits in a succession of ever more ambitious experiments. Perhaps the most popular complement in the world today is the frothy steam-whipped milk that goes to make the Italian "cappuccino".

Caffeine

In the course of about three centuries, in the Western world over 90 per cent of the adult population has become converted to coffee, for two reasons: firstly it is an excellent beverage, and secondly it does you good or makes you feel better.

There are over 1,200 chemical components present in coffee, very many of which help to give it the taste and aroma we enjoy, but one in particular – caffeine – has physiological effects on our bodies. Ever since the 17th century the therapeutic properties of coffee have been known and put to use, for example in the treatment of gout and

pellagra. Today these are no longer the maladies that worry humanity, but coffee continues to perform its beneficial action as a stimulant to digestion and peristalsis, promoting pancreatic and diuretic activity, and having a regulating and stimulating action on the cardiovascular system. Its most important action however is the action of caffeine on the central nervous system: it increases awareness, improves concentration and memory, speeds up response to external stimuli (reflexes) and, according to the most recent research, it appears to have a significant positive influence on mood.

So, what is this caffeine that can do such wonders? Chemically it is an alkaloid, 1,3,7-trimethylxanthine to be precise: it is an odorless, bitter white powder, soluble in water. In fact it is almost completely dissolved in water in the various methods of coffee-making, with the exception of the espresso method: because of the limited amount of water used in this method and the short time in which the coffee is in contact with the water (about 30 seconds), not all the caffeine is dissolved, particularly if the espresso is extra-strong (25-30 cc). The fact that caffeine has so many beneficial effects should not lead to its being taken in excess: although it is only

Left: A transparent espresso "extraction" chamber, for the experimental observation of the complex physical phenomena that take place during the passage of the water. *Below:* The curves show that an average metabolizer of caffeine can drink more of the Arabica species (green curve) than the Robusta species (brown curve), because of the former's lower caffeine content.

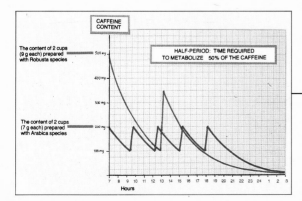

dangerous at very high levels (10 grams, corresponding to almost 100 cups of espresso), the ideal quantity for an adult is an average of 300-400 milligrams a day, equal to 4 small cups of espresso made with coffee of the Arabica species. It should not be forgotten that this species contains from 1.1 to 1.7 per cent of caffeine, whereas the Robusta species contains 2 to 4.5 per cent, nor that one cup of espresso uses 6-7 grams of coffee as against the 10-15 grams for a cup of coffee made by the other methods.

Moreover not all individuals metabolize caffeine at the same rate: on average, 20 per cent of caffeine present in the circulation metabolizes every hour, but there are great variations from one individual to another. Women are generally faster than men except during pregnancy, when the metabolic rate slows down to such an extent that coffee may be inadvisable at this time. Caffeine is inadvisable for anyone suffering from gastritis, gastroduodenal ulcers or cardio-circulatory disorders. To know what our individual intake should be, we have to know whether we metabolize caffeine slowly or quickly, and remember that the amount of caffeine differs between the two species of coffee. Our own body, with its efficient system of

autodiagnosis, soon tells us how many cups of coffee we can drink to derive the maximum benefit and satisfaction.

In any case it is better to take small quantities of caffeine several times a day than greater quantities concentrated in few cups. This explains the success of espresso coffee: its caffeine content is lower than that of coffee made by other methods (90-150 mg per cup as against 150-300 mg) and it is also suitable for drinking several times a day between meals.

De-caffeinated coffee

Disregarding any thirst-quenching quality of coffee, which can be discounted if it is made by methods such as espresso or "Turkish", there are still two reasons why people drink coffee: for pleasure, and for its physiological effects.

Chiefly responsible for these effects is caffeine, a nervotonic substance that should not however be consumed in unlimited quantities, and which is altogether inadvisable for those suffering from certain conditions (cardio-circulatory and gastric disorders). It is hard to do without the pleasure that coffee gives, so the solution is simply to avoid the caffeine.

Early this century de-caffeinated coffee was introduced, so that people who cannot

It takes an average of about two hours to halve the amount of caffeine taken into the system. The curves show the different times required by a slow metabolizer to assimilate a preparation made of Arabica and Robusta, and one of just the Arabica species.

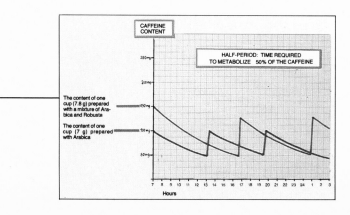

Open-air café in Turkey. The preparation of "Turkish coffee" requires care. Many cafés have a heated container with a layer of sand spread on the bottom of it. The "ibriks" are filled with water and powdered coffee and buried in this sand. The traditional rule when making Turkish coffee is that it has to be brought to a boil three times before being served.

tolerate caffeine or those who have already drunk their "ideal" intake for the day can still enjoy coffee. At this point someone may object that if de-caffeinated coffee should be consumed because it is "good", how is it that it so often isn't? There are two answers: the first is that perhaps many coffee-roasters do not see the argument for excluding caffeine. The second, more objectively, is that de-caffeinated coffee tends not to keep so well, and so loses its quality. In fact the most common de-caffeination process incorporates the use of solvents (dichloromethane or ethyl acetate) which not only dissolve the caffeine but also the heavy oils called "waxes" (the chemical name is sterols). These substances, which are concentrated in the outer cells of the bean, occlude its pores, slowing down the loss of gases from inside the bean. These gases, mainly carbon dioxide, prevent oxygen from reaching the interior of the cells, so preventing oxidizations of the substances inside and slowing down deterioration in the quality of the coffee. In the absence of these waxes, deterioration is more rapid. This requires that these de-caffeinated coffees be consumed within a shorter period, but because they are less in demand the turnover is slower than normal. You should therefore check the expiry date or, if it is shown, the packing date.

In the process of de-caffeination with solvents, the green coffee must first be given preparatory steam treatment at about 120°, to open the cell pores so that the solvent can penetrate. The caffeine dissolved by the solvent is subsequently isolated and recovered: it is generally bought by pharmaceutical industries for use in the preparation of various drugs. The coffee is then washed and dried, after which it is ready for roasting.

Some consumers are worried about the traces of solvents that remain in the coffee: fortunately they are only present in minimal amounts, which are controlled by law (in Italy they must not exceed 15 parts per million in roasted coffee). There are two other ways of removing the caffeine: the "oldest" is repeated washing in water, which takes a long time and is not very efficient. Water is not a "selective" solvent: as well as the caffeine it removes other soluble substances such as sugars and proteins. The most recent method in place of solvents uses liquid carbon dioxide: this acts selectively on the caffeine, that is to say it releases the alkaloid and nothing else. From the point of view of quality this is the ideal method, but unfor-

Right: Breakfast in an old hotel dining room. The world can be divided into two groups: those who drink coffee, and those who drink tea. This division is most clearly demostrated at breakfast. Mediterraneans traditionally take advantage of caffeine's ability to transform body fat into sugar (and, therefore, energy) by just having coffee for breakfast, without having anything else.

tunately the machinery required entails a huge investment, so it is still relatively rare. Whatever method is used, the loss of quality due to de-caffeination is imperceptible: even an expert taster may have difficulty in distinguishing between de-caffeinated and "normal" coffee. Generally the flavour is less bitter (caffeine has a bitter taste) so the sweet flavour becomes more dominant. Technically therefore we can produce de-caffeinated coffee blends

that are as good as normal blends: everything depends on the quality of the coffees used. You reap what you sow.

World coffee producers and consumers
The nations of the world can be divided into tea-drinkers or coffee-drinkers. Everywhere these two beverages are in competition, and although coffee- and tea-drinkers are frequently found in the same place, and indeed in the same family, one or other of

One can hardly imagine any restaurant or bar not serving coffee. Some more refined places offer the customer a choice of blends, types, and even different ways of preparation. The customer can therefore select which type of coffee goes best with his particular choice of dessert. *Below:* An old coffee pot.

these rival beverages is always clearly the favourite. Paradoxically this is also the case even in coffee-producing countries. Whilst we may not be astonished that in India, a leading producer of tea and medium producer of coffee (over 2 million bags a year), annual coffee consumption is only a few grams per head, it is surprising that the same is true of most African countries where coffee is their main source of wealth.

The exceptions are the Ivory Coast which produces over 4 million bags a year and where per capita consumption is about 0.4 kg, and Ethiopia where over 3 million bags of "cultivated" beans are harvested each year (it is estimated that as many grow wild) and local consumption is over 3 kg per head.

This is close to that of Western consumer countries; to find a comparable consumption among "producers" we have to go to the Americas.

The leading world producer, Brazil, is also the second among consumers, with 3.5 kg per head per year. The second producer is

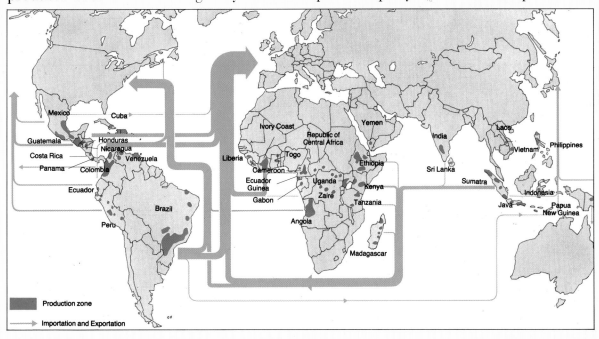

The map shows all the coffee-producing countries and the importation-exportation routes. It is interesting to note that all of these countries are located between the Tropic of Cancer and the Tropic of Capricorn. Coffee is also drunk in these producing countries. The yearly amount per capita ranges from 6 kg for Costa Rica to just a few grams for India and the African countries. The greatest interest in coffee-drinking, as regards the producing countries, is shown in Central and South America.

countries coffee is usually made by the infusion method; the coffee is medium-roast, medium-ground. Generally about 10 grams of coffee are used per cup; normally it is not a blend but coffee of the same species and variety grown locally (it would be absurd to import coffee from other places to blend it!). Sometimes the percolation method is used and occasionally also the espresso method; in Brazil, for example, it is not difficult to find espresso coffee in the large cities, in place of the *cafesiño*, which is a very strong infusion. The quality of the coffee consumed in producer countries is not always satisfactory, for at least two reasons.

The first is that the highest quality coffees are reserved for export, as they fetch the highest prices; the second is that it is not possible to balance the flavour and aroma of "pure" coffees as can be done by blending different coffees.

In consumer countries on the other hand we find a wider range of blends, roasts, methods of making coffee and ways of drinking it. Each has adapted coffee to its own culture and customs, and more specifically to its own drinking habits: so

Colombia, with more than 12 million bags a year; the Colombians too are leading consumers, with about 4 kg per head. However the prize goes to Costa Rica, with annual production touching 2 million bags, and annual consumption running at 6 kg per head. Other nations of Central America are also good consumers: El Salvador and Guatemala (each producing over 2.5 million bags) with a consumption of nearly 3 kg per person; Nicaragua

Whatever the occasion and whatever the company, coffee is always very welcome, as in the case of the two cowboys shown *above* who live in the hot Texas territory, or the women shown *below* who pour themselves a cup of coffee between ski runs. Hot coffee is welcome in any sort of weather. If the weather gets too hot, some people prefer their coffee iced.

in some countries people drink coffee to quench their thirst as well as for its stimulant properties, while in others they drink it so strong (made with little water) that it is more like an elixir.

To return to the dichotomy of "tea or coffee drinkers", we can classify Great Britain (together with Japan, Russia and so on) as being predominantly a nation of tea-drinkers; the other European countries are predominantly coffee-drinkers, together with the United States where coffee has come to be regarded as the national beverage.

The highest per capita annual consumption figures are to be found in Northern Europe, in Scandinavia, where they exceed 12 kg.

In Denmark they drop to 11 kg, in Holland to 9, in Belgium and Austria to 8, in Germany to 7, and in France and Switzerland to 6. In the United States consumption is about 4.6 kg (it was considerably higher in the seventies); next come Italy (where they regard themselves as very heavy coffee-drinkers) and Canada with about 4.3 kg. Consumption then drops steeply to about 2 kg in Greece, Yugoslavia, Spain, Great Britain, Australia and Japan.

This is also the level of consumption in Hungary, while in other Eastern European countries it drops to below 1 kg.

There is a connection between level of consumption and method of preparation: where the percolation method is common, as in Northern Europe, consumption is higher.

This is probably due to the fact that more water is used to make coffee in this way, so that it also serves as a thirst-quenching

Above: A girl having a cup of coffee in a French outdoor café. While the drinking of espresso coffee was once confined to quite a small geographical area, extensive tourism and business travel have extended the limits of the appreciation of espresso coffee to all the globe.

drink. In fact it is not unusual in Nordic countries for a large cup of coffee to be served with meals. Percolated coffee is rarely drunk by itself: in the morning it accompanies the copious "continental" breakfast, at midday it is served with a slice of tart or a cake or biscuits. Those who drink espresso or "Turkish" coffee however usually only consume it with food at breakfast (not a widespread custom in Mediterranean countries).

There is another interesting connection between the quantity and quality of the coffees consumed in the various countries. The most common index of the quality of coffee is grade 4 for Colombian, 3 for Other Milds, 2 for Brazilian and other Arabica and 1 for Robusta, these values taking into consideration the percentage of the various types of coffee imported over a given period.

Generally a high grade of quality is matched by high consumption, while low quality is matched by low consumption. Thus for several years we find Finland ranking first in both lists, whereas Italy and Great Britain, with their low indices of quality, come last in the European list of consumers. As is always the case, there are exceptions that prove the rule: France generally has a lower index of quality than Italy, whereas its consumption is markedly higher (almost one and a half times as much).

High quality coffees increase consumption not only because they are more satisfying to the palate but because of the effect of their caffeine content. We may in fact recall that Robustas contain from 2 to 4.5 per cent whereas Arabicas contain from 1.1 to 1.7 per cent, so you can drink more of the latter without thereby taking more caffeine.

Methods of making coffee

The substances in coffee that man appreciates for their stimulant properties and for their flavour and aroma are those which are released in boiling water: this is why the Arabs long ago learned to make a hot beverage with roasted coffee. In this way they could extract the best from the coffee without also getting the solid substances that are insoluble in water, such as cellulose, which have a less pleasant taste and smell. The substances responsible for the taste of the infusion (bitter, sweet, acid) are mainly those that are soluble in water: sugars, caffeine, proteins, chlorogenic acids, etc., whilst those that give coffee its aroma (or perfume, that we discern with our

Side: A beautiful porcelain coffee service which is suitable for either percolated or brewed coffee. *Right:* Eduardo De Filippo – the famous actor – and his equally famous "tazzulella" or "little cup". Being a true Neapolitan. De Filippo worshipped coffee. His description of how the Neapolitans used to roast the beans on their balconies prior to grinding them to use in making their famous black Neapolitan espresso was so vivid that the listener could smell the roasting. hear the grinding and taste the coffee.

olfactory sense) are almost entirely insoluble. These are the coffee oils to which the volatile aromas (present in the cells of roasted coffee in the gaseous state) tend to attach themselves.

Part of these fatty substances, whilst they cannot dissolve in water, are made more fluid at high temperatures and "float" on the surface of the infusion. It is only with the espresso method that the oils (together with other insoluble substances called colloids) can be emulsified in water in appreciable quantities, giving the beverage its incomparable aroma and "body".

The scene is Berlin in the summer of 1955. The sign says: "Traditions are not dead here. Families can make their own coffee!" It is difficult to say what Germans prefer best, beer or coffee, but a considerable number of them are going over to espresso.

There are two main ways of "extracting" the most valued substances from coffee: maceration and percolation. With either method, the coffee must first be ground, to increase its surface contact with the hot water.

In the first method the ground coffee is put into boiling water and left to steep for at least five minutes: this gives an "infusion" which is then strained to remove the grounds. The Melior method uses a strainer with a metallic mesh which is pressed down with a plunger to separate the coffee grounds from the infusion.

"Turkish" coffee is made using a variation of the same method: ground coffee and sugar are boiled in the water (the rule says three times consecutively). After the third boiling the pot is left to stand until all the grounds have settled on the bottom, and the coffee is then ready for drinking. To ensure that no particles are left floating, the coffee is very finely ground, which breaks up all its cells, releasing the gases they contain. All types of coffee are suitable for the steeping method; it is generally a fairly light roast and coffee which results is quite rich, heavy, with plenty of body, especially if a small amount of water is used.

The percentage of substances (almost all soluble in water) extracted from coffee by steeping, with or without boiling, is about 20 per cent. Coffee made in this way is quite aromatic, because a small percentage of oils (the "vectors" or carriers of the volatile aromas) is released into the water, floating on the surface.

The second method of making coffee, the percolation method, consists of passing boiling (or nearly boiling) water through the ground coffee.

The water may drip through the coffee driven simply by its own weight (through gravity), as is the case with the "Napoletana" machine, or by slight pressure provided by steam (unlikely to exceed one atmosphere), as is the case with "Mocha" coffee, or else by the high pressure (9-10 atmospheres) produced mechanically and hydraulically in the espresso coffee machine.

The greater the pressure on the water, the less time it takes to drip through the coffee: percolated coffee takes a few minutes, Mocha takes only about a minute, and the espresso machine about 30 seconds. Percolated coffee is very common in Northern Europe and North America: the machines for making it, for example the German Melitta or the American Bun-o-matic, are quite simple and can make

Side: A small coffee-maker for preparing percolated coffee at home. During the last few years, the use of these coffee-makers – which greatly simplify and speed up the making of percolated coffee – has become almost as widespread as the use of the home-type, espresso-coffee machines. The percolated coffee-maker also generally produces hot water for tea or other brews.

from 2 to 12 cups at a time, according to the different models. They consist of a glass or metal or plastic cone with a hole at the bottom that leads to the coffee jug, which is generally made of glass. A cone of filter paper is placed inside the cone before putting in the coffee, medium-ground.

The appropriate amount of boiling water may be heated separately or automatically brought to the boil by the machine itself, and is then dripped onto the ground coffee in the cone. The water dissolves the soluble substances as it passes through the coffee, hence also passing through the filter paper which retains any smaller particles of coffee, and then through the hole at the bottom of the cone into the jug.

The beverage is then ready for drinking, and if not wanted immediately is kept at the same temperature by the hot-plate on which the jug stands. However if coffee is left to stand for too long it loses a lot of its aroma (which is not very strong to begin with, as few oils manage to get through the filter paper); if the coffee is not used within half an hour it is better to make some fresh.

To make percolated coffee, "washed" Arabica blends are generally used as their hard consistency is such that they do not produce too much impalpable fine powder that would block the pores of the filter paper and impede the infusion from passing through. For the same reason, and to facilitate the flow of water, the light-roast blend is also coarsely ground. For these reasons, this method only extracts 20 per cent of the soluble substances from the coffee. The result is a light, diluted coffee, sweet and slightly acidulous, with a pleasing aroma (providing good quality coffees are used) but bland.

The "Mocha" method is also fairly simple: it consists of three interrelated parts. The bowl at the base is filled with water for heating, in the middle is the metal filter containing the ground coffee, and the upper bowl is filled by the water as it is forced up by the pressure of the steam through the coffee so it becomes an infusion. Mocha coffee can be made with blends containing all types of coffee, medium to dark roast, and ideally fairly fine ground.

The filter gets filled with grounds and it is better not to press on it since, if there is too much pressure on the rising water, too much pressure develops in the lower bowl, causing too high a temperature; overheated water gives coffee a rather unpleasant "burnt" taste. Another way to avoid

The so-called "mocha" coffee-maker is the one most found in Italian homes. This unit could be considered the connecting link between the percolator and espresso types of coffee-makers. The water comes to a boil, moves upward through a tube, and is then forced down (under low pressure) through a cup packed with finely-ground coffee. The result is a sort of compromise between the characteristics of percolated and espresso coffee.

Top: Two "mocha" models. The one on the left is made of aluminium, while the one on the right is a steel-copper model made by Alessi. *Above left:* With this "Melior" type of coffee-maker, water is first added and brought to a boil. Then the coffee powder is added and maceration is allowed to take place for a few minutes. The handle (at the top of unit) is then pushed to force the coffee grounds all the way down. *Right:* The so-called "Neapolitan" coffee-maker ranks second in Italian popularity after the "mocha".

this happening is to lower the heat as soon as the first drops of coffee appear in the upper bowl.

By this method as much as 22 per cent of the substances contained in the coffee are extracted.

The resultant beverage has a strong, definite concentrated flavour, on the bitter side; it is medium-bodied, with a fairly strong aroma, both because of the darker roast and the fact that the oils are forced through under the light pressure so that they float in the infusion in the upper bowl of the coffee-maker. Because of its strong taste, Mocha coffee is generally sweetened with sugar and often taken with a dash of milk, whereas percolated coffee is also taken "neat", or possibly with light or heavy cream.

Espresso coffee

The third variation of this drip or percolation method is based on water that is not so hot (about 90°C) being forced through the ground coffee under high pressure, and is known as espresso. Coffees made by either of the methods mentioned previously look very similar and differ only slightly in flavour and aroma: espresso coffee is another thing altogether! It is a marvel of chemical and physical engineering which extracts all that is best from the coffee and no more.

Like everything extraordinary it shows a high level of complexity, from its transformation to its final structure. Espresso in fact is at once a solution (of sugars, caffeine, acids, proteins, etc.), an emulsion (of oils and colloids) and a suspension (of impalpable particles of coffee cells and minute bubbles of gas), all concentrated within a few cubic centimetres' volume (20 for a strong espresso) and covered with thick hazel-coloured "cream" or "foam".

When we taste espresso coffee, in addition to its higher density, we are at once struck by its concentrated flavour and especially by its aromas, which distinguish it from coffee made by other methods. Aroma and body are the two dimensions which espresso coffee adds to the flavour, the main feature of other kinds of coffee. Because the water passes through the coffee under high pressure, the coffee may – and indeed should – be fine-ground, thereby increasing surface contact with the water and favouring the extraction of the soluble substances which give coffee its flavour.

Again because of this high pressure about 10 per cent of the coffee oils may be

Right: An array of cups being kept warm while waiting to be filled with fragrant espresso coffee. When it comes out of the machine, the temperature of the espresso is almost 80°C. The ideal espresso cup has just the right mass for removing the excess heat while keeping the temperature of the espresso constant during the time it takes to drink it. If the cup is too light, it will not be able to absorb sufficient initial heat. If it is too heavy, it will absorb too much heat.

emulsified: as the volatile aromas tend to attach themselves after roasting to these fatty substances, this explains the aromatic quality of espresso coffee. The oils are also partly responsible for the body of the coffee, and in particular what might be called its smooth or "velvety" texture. The high viscosity of espresso coffee is very important because associated with it is a lower surface tension, so that the liquid can penetrate the taste buds more deeply and consequently increase our perception of flavour.

The body also depends on the presence of tiny bubbles of gas (mainly carbon dioxide) in suspension and on emulsified colloids. The latter also have the property of inhibiting the receptors of bitter tastes in the gustatory papillae: this explains why even though espresso coffee has a very strong flavour, it almost never tastes too bitter. The combined action of the colloids and the oils emulsified in tiny drops is furthermore responsible for what is known as the "after-flavour": by lowering the surface tension of the liquid the colloids also allow the tiny drops of oil to penetrate deeply into the gustatory papillae where the oil settles and slowly releases the aromatic substances that had become fixed to it.

These aromas are perceived by our olfactory system during exhalation even up to ten minutes and more after drinking the espresso. Such perfection must be "protected" during the moments that elapse between preparation and consumption: this protection is afforded by the layer of "cream" which impedes loss of heat and above all of aroma before the espresso is consumed.

The secrets of making a good espresso
The literal meaning of the word "espresso" is "made on the spur of the moment". It is an adjective applied to foods and

Above: The "Illetta" was the first coffee-making machine that automatically measured the water. It was built in 1935 by Francesco Illy (*below*) and had a real market innovation: water pressure not produced by heat. Up to that time, the water was heated to produce the steam required to pressurize the water. If more pressure was required, more steam pressure had to be produced, and this took more heat. This extra-heat tended to "burn" the coffee. The "Illetta" used compressed air to provide the required pressure.

168

drinks that are made at the moment of asking, and in Italy is chiefly used to describe coffee, so that it has become a noun: when you ask for "an espresso" in a bar or restaurant it always means a coffee.

This new method of making coffee was at the end of the 19th century (the first machine was shown at the Paris Fair in 1855) to overcome the drawbacks of the other methods, in particular the time they take (several minutes) and the consequent loss af aroma when the coffee is kept hot instead of being consumed immediately. The new machine had to be able to make one or two coffees at a time quickly, so that the customer only had to wait a few moments to be served. In order to make the water pass more speedily through the measured amount of ground coffee, the inventors had the idea of putting the water under pressure. Initially this pressure was provided by the steam that the barman skillfully regulated by means of various taps: making espresso coffee in those days was a real art.

The first manufacturer of espresso machines was Bezzerra (1901), followed in the next 50 years by seven other Italians and two Frenchmen.

In 1935 Francesco Illy substituted compressed air for steam, so producing the first automatic machine.

All the trade models at that time were rather complicated, expensive and difficult to operate: they were to be found in "pioneering" establishments, used to attract a larger clientele. Things changed in 1945, the date of the introduction of the Gaggia machine. Its concept drastically simplified the design and action of the espresso machine, the pressure being provided by a large spring, previously "loaded" by means of a lever. The spring drives a piston which in turn compresses the water.

To this day in some areas of Southern Italy these "lever" machines are preferred to the other models for the quality of the espresso they produce. In the 50's the lever models, sold by various manufacturers, conquered the market in Italian bars and restaurants.

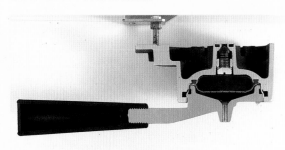

At the end of the '70s, Ernesto Illy came up with another idea. It was called the "Espresso System". The cutaway above shows the "extraction" chamber in which the dosage of ground coffee was placed, pressed and closed in by two layers of filter paper. The advantage of the "Espresso System" was that a good quality of espresso coffee could be made, regardless of the operator's expertise, or the facility with which the coffee-making unit could be used and maintained.

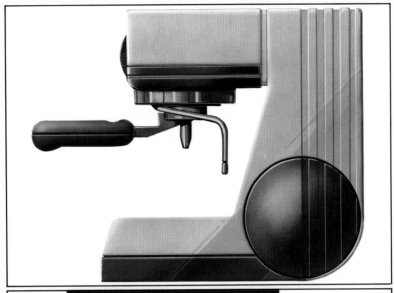

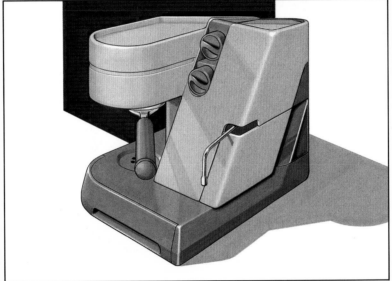

The little espresso coffee-making machines have come to form part of the beautiful, sophisticated kitchen décor found in many homes today. They have proved to be very attractive in any type of kitchen. The importance of esthetics has placed great emphasis on design as well as on the technical aspects. *Left and above:* Some models by Studio Giugiaro Design.

Another great innovation followed at the end of the decade: Ernesto Valente, who had produced the Faema (1950), had the idea of replacing the spring of the lever machine with a rotating pump driven by a small electric motor.

As it was not possible to work the pump with hot water, Valente decided to compress the water while it was still cold, before passing it into the heat exchanger in the boiler of the machine. Whereas previously the water had been first heated and then compressed, from now on the order was reversed.

Thus in 1961 came the first model of the "continuous delivery" machines, the famed Faema E 61 of which hundreds are still in use.

Today it is the model most commonly used, both in public places and at home; other available models are the lever type and the "hydraulic" model, in which the piston itself, instead of the spring, is driven by the water pressure in the tubes. To make a good espresso, however, it is not enough to have a good machine: there are in fact four basic elements.

The first is the blend itself, the second is the measured amount of coffee, then comes the machine and lastly the operator who has to regulate and control the other three elements so that they interact correctly.

The importance of the blend
In creating an espresso blend one has several aims, which concern the flavour and aroma wished. The flavour must above all be balanced and harmonious; sweetness is prized above all (everyone likes it), the balance between bitter and acid must be adjusted to suit the taste of the majority of consumers, which varies from one area to another. Aroma pleases everyone, so it must be maximised, not only in terms of quantity but in terms of quality. The aroma should be pleasing,

A cup of espresso coffee made with the beans of the Arabica species has a light-brown color with reddish highlights. On the other hand, the Robusta species is a dark-brown coffee with grey highlights. Moreover, it has larger, thicker bubbles which, however, disappear rather rapidly. One raw and one roasted bean for each of the two species are shown next to the cups of coffee.

with a broad spectrum of characteristic components, to give the blend an unmistakeable personality of its own. Lastly, attention must be paid to the body of the blend: full-bodied coffee is the measure of a good blend and correct preparation.

To obtain these results the coffee roasting firm adjusts two elements: the composition of the blend and the degree of the roast. A number of different coffees go into the blend, each of which has its own unique and inimitable organoleptic properties.

So to obtain the best result consistently, samples of each consignment of coffee are tested, blended together so that there is a balanced flavour and aroma, and the composition of the blend is "withdrawn"

Glass cups of roasted beans in a drying chamber awaiting laboratory tests. Roasted coffee beans are hygroscopic. The moisture absorbed from the air changes their physical structure and makes them less brittle. For this reason, the degree of grindability of the coffee beans has to be adjusted to the particular climatic and atmospheric conditions of the moment.

every time a new consignment of coffee is used. This "consistent results" method is not dissimilar to the combining of wines in champagne production.

However the most common method is the "fixed components" method which consists of establishing a particular blend as described above and then reproducing it by always using consignments of coffee from the same source and blending them together in the same proportions. It is a simpler procedure but the quality of the blend is less consistent. To give a general idea of the ideal composition of an espresso blend, we can start by dividing coffee into three groups: Arabica natural, Arabica washed and Robusta. Robusta coffees, as well as being less expensive, have one particular advantage: they give espresso a lot of body. However this quality is cancelled out by such drawbacks as their higher caffeine content, more bitter flavour and lack of aroma (often "woody" or "earthy"), so that it is inadvisable to use them. The ideal blend is therefore composed of Arabica natural and Arabica washed: the former (ideally Brazilian Santos) have a balanced flavour and a medium-strength, wide range of aroma, and form the ideal basis in percentages that can exceed 50 per cent.

Arabica washed are generally sweeter and more acid; they have a very strong but relatively narrow range of aroma, that may be flowery or fruity, sometimes with a pleasant scent of toast.

Too high a proportion of Arabica washed must not be used, for two reasons: their characteristic acidity is heightened in the preparation of espresso coffee, and their consistency is often very hard and tenacious; after grinding, the particles are still highly homogeneous. In order to encourage the macromolecules of the colloids to pass through (which is so important to give the coffee body) it is therefore better to have particles of different sizes in the ground coffee, as occurs with Arabica natural.

Roasting the blend for espresso coffee may be done at quite high temperatures, which release the maximum aroma.

The more pronounced bitter flavour associated with dark-roast coffee is not a problem, as it is "neutralized" by the colloids which, in addition to giving body, inhibit the receptors of bitter taste in the taste buds.

To meet consumer preference, which varies from one latitude to another, roasting is done to different degrees, from medium roast in Northern Italy to dark

Right: This small roaster used coal as a heat source, but similar types have also used wood. Today, heating is supplied by natural gas, fuel oil or electricity. The machine shown in the photo is full of roasted beans whose volume has increased about 50 per cent during the roasting process.

roast in the South. In general the darker roasts are preferred where more concentrated espresso is served: the increased bitterness is offset by a higher concentration of colloids.

Coffee grinder and dispenser

The main function of the coffee-grinder/dispenser is to crush the roasted bean into smaller particles, to increase the surface contact of the coffee with the hot water so helping the soluble substances to dissolve.

The grains should not be too fine, however, or they would block the flow of water: there should also be sufficient space between them to allow the macro-molecules of emulsified colloids to escape into the water. In short, ground coffee should be composed of certain proportions of different grain sizes; that is to say it should include sizes ranging from fine powder to coarse grains almost a millimetre in diameter.

It is only in this way that the right compromise can be achieved between surface contact, resistance to water flow and enough space between the grains to allow the colloids through.

The difficult task of achieving this result is entrusted to special rollers: they may be flat or conical and are made of tempered steel forged so as to create sharp "teeth" which crack the bean and then cut it to the proper degree of fineness. The distance between the rollers can be adjusted to give the desired grind, coarse or medium or fine.

As there is no "precise" method of determining the correct degree of grind (which anyway varies from one machine to another), the operator must rely on the empirical method of trial and error.

The rule for espresso is that it should be made with 6-7 grams of coffee, with water at 90 °C and at 9-10 atmospheres, in about 30 seconds' time (20 for domestic machines): if it takes longer, this means that the grind is too fine and so must be

Above: An old print showing women preparing coffee with the use of hand-operated grinders. *Side:* A rather elaborate manually-operated grinder. This is still the best way to grind coffee beans at home, because there is no danger of the conical mills overheating and thus ruining the beans.

made coarser. If on the other hand it takes a shorter time, the grind is too coarse and must be made finer. It is not possible to say exactly how much coarser or finer it should be: this must be established by trial and error.

The rollers, which are the heart of the coffee-grinder, are eventually affected by wear and tear and so must be replaced from time to time: more frequently if they are flat and small in diameter, less fre-

quently if they are larger in diameter or else conical (some can grind more than 1000 kg of coffee).

After grinding, the ground coffee falls into the dispenser, which delivers the correct quantity to make an espresso. The amount is determined by volume and can usually be regulated: to determine the correct measure, the volume of ground coffee delivered by the dispenser must be placed on a pair of scales and translated

A French couple preparing coffee. The gentleman is using a stopwatch to time the operation! The coffee-maker in this photograph used the "mocha" principle, except that the water was heated apart in an electrical boiler. The boiler was separate from the extraction chamber. Similar models were also used in Italy, but were soon replaced by the "mocha", which cost a lot less and was much easier to use.

into weight. Changes of blend or of degree of grind, which alter the specific weight of the ground coffee, mean that the amount delivered by the dispenser must be checked and regulated so as to maintain a consistent weight. In practice the degree of grind and the quantity dispensed are checked and regulated daily, since the quality of an espresso also depends on their being correct.

The espresso machine

The job of the espresso machine is to provide energy to the water that must pass through the ground coffee "capturing" the best substances. It has two ways of providing this energy: heat and pressure. They are produced from separate sources, so that each can be precisely controlled: this is the secret of the espresso method. The heat supplied to the water does not even bring it to boiling point (the correct temperature is about 90 °C), whereas the pressure applied is rather high, 9-10 atmospheres. The most common source of heat is an electrical resistor in the heater; alternatively gas is sometimes used.

The pressure is usually generated by an electric pump or else by the thrust of a "loaded" spring or by the thrust of the water from the mains amplified by a system of pistons of different diameters. The heart of the espresso machine, and the most accessible part, is where the measured amount of the ground coffee is dispensed into a filter with a flat base perforated with a lot of tiny holes. The water enters via the top of the filter, evenly distributed by a small "shower", at the correct temperature and pressure. The water passes through the coffee dissolving the soluble substances and certain gases (chiefly carbon dioxide) and emulsifying the colloids and the oils. When the liquid reaches the holes at the bottom of the filter expansion causes the dissolved gases to be released and these, together with emulsified substances, form the tiny bubbles that characterise the "cream" on the surface of the espresso. Beneath the filter the coffee runs into the filter holder from which it is distributed to the coffee cups through one or two spouts.

All these parts of the machine must be thoroughly cleaned every day, for they are the parts in direct contact with the coffee. Like the pump, they are also subject to wear and tear, so must periodically be inspected and replaced as necessary. Water softeners are used to prevent lime scale, but for small domestic espresso machines flat (not gassy!) mineral water with a low

Two epochs are compared here. *Left:* In the '30s, thanks to the new copper and brass commercial coffee-makers, espresso coffee became very popular with the public. *Side:* Beginning with the '70s, the appearance of the little espresso coffee-maker for the home marked the beginning of a brilliant future for this little gem.

content of mineral salts may be used for making the coffee: as the quality of the water is superior, it also makes a better coffee.

The human touch

With the early espresso machines, which worked by steam pressure, the human factor played a vital role; but even today, with all the technological refinements, the skill of the operator is still of great importance. The application of new technologies to the espresso machine has made it easier and in some cases quicker to make the coffee, but its quality still depends at least 50 per cent on the skill of the operator who at best is a real "master".

He has three jobs to do: he must choose the right blend and grind of coffee and determine the correct amount to be dispensed, he must choose the right machine and check that it is working properly and keep it clean, and lastly he actually makes the espresso. Only if the blend and grind are correct and the right machine is used can a good espresso be made: he must therefore choose carefully, consider the various alternatives and bear in mind not only the quality and reliability of all these items but also whether the manufacturer of the machine offers advice and whether he will

service the machine. He must keep a constant check on the weight of the amount of coffee released by the dispenser (between 6 and 7 grams) and the degree of grind (such that the water comes through in 20-30 seconds); the temperature (between 88 and 92 °C) and the pressure (9-10 atmospheres) of the water.

If any one of these is outside the norm he must regulate the machine or ask for it to be serviced.

Some parts of the equipment must be cleaned periodically: the container that holds the coffee beans and the dispenser of the ground coffee should be cleaned every week; the filters, the filter holders and the spouts should be cleaned every day. Some of these parts, as we have mentioned, are subject to wear and tear, in particular the grinders, the filters and the spouts which need replacing from time to time. In addition to attending to all these tasks, the operator must also supply fresh water-softener if this is used.

After this he only has to follow a few easy steps in making the espresso: 1) always keep the filter holder in place so that it stays hot; 2) thoroughly remove the grounds of the previous coffee from the filter holder; 3) release the correct amount of coffee by pulling the small lever on the

A cutaway view of the delivery of a home espresso-maker. Except for the filter and the filter holder (which have to hold the same amount of ground coffee), the boiler (or heat-exchanger), pump and body are miniaturized copies of those used in commercial models.

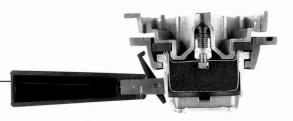

dispenser and allowing it to return to place of its own accord without holding it – the lever, which is worked by a spring, will thus give a "tap" on the dispenser that guarantees that the full measure of coffee is released; 4) press firmly on the coffee in the filter, perhaps using a tamping tool which must have a flat base and be kept level with the base of the filter; 5) wipe the edges of the filter before attaching it; 6) use cups that are hot and not too large; 7) as soon as the filter holder is in place start the machine working; 8) even if the machine is automatic, keep an eye on the cups to make sure that they are filled to the desired level (the flow from the two spouts is not always equal).

In short, the Maestro of the Espresso must

The espresso "machine" (as it is called) also has an important role in the railroad station, as can be seen by the prominent position taken by the new Gaggia machine sitting on the counter. Gaggia is credited with having rapidly promoted the drinking of espresso after the war by developing this simple and easy-to-use coffee-making "machine".

measured amounts of ground coffee which can be inserted in special espresso machines designed to hold them. The Nestlè single measure of coffee is in a foil sachet while the Illycaffè version is closely packed and sealed between two layers of filter paper. Using either of these, espresso coffee is made so easily that no skill or effort are required on the part of the operator, and the cleaning and maintenance of the machine will be minimal. And so, making an espresso, that highly complex concentration of tastes and aromas, is becoming the easiest thing in the world.

Drinking coffee: the sense of sight, smell, taste... and touch
When drinking espresso almost all our senses apart from the sense of hearing come into play. Our appreciation and enjoyment are the synthesis of the signals sent to our brain by the senses of sight, smell, taste and touch. Generally, as with wine-tasting, this is the sequence of the senses that we use when tasting espresso. It is the sight or visual inspection of the "cream" on the surface of the espresso that prepares us for the strength of the coffee and gives an indication of the blend. A pale cream, of homogeneous colour tending to whitish yellow, signifies that the coffee has

take great pains, but his satisfaction will be equally great when he serves a perfect espresso to his customers.
Recently some firms (Nestlè and Illycaffè) have perfected a new idea to help the operator, namely individual sachets of

The cutaway shows the "espresso system" at work. No particular skill is required to use the system, yet a perfect cup of espresso is made each and every time. A great deal of research was necessary to develop this system, because the ideal shape for the coffee portion had to be found, as well as its thickness, the density, and the required amount and distribution of the ground coffee.

been under-extracted: the temperature and/or pressure of the water is too low or the extraction time too short (either because too small a measure of coffee is dispensed or because the coffee is too coarsely ground). If the colour of the cream is tinged with dark brown (almost black) on the one side and white on the other, this means that the espresso is over-extracted: water temperature and/or pressure are too high or the extraction time is too long (because too large a measure of coffee is dispensed or because the coffee is too finely ground). Correct extraction produces a cream of homogeneous colour, at best dappled with darker streaks. If the colour is deep hazel with reddish tints, and the bubbles are tiny and compact, this signifies that the blend is composed mainly or exclusively of coffees of the Arabica

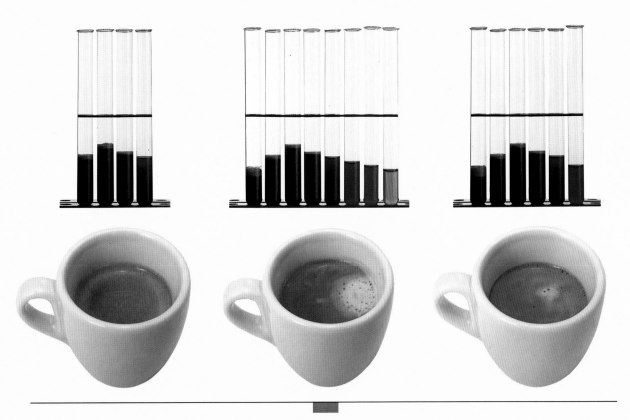

To obtain the best espresso coffee, the extraction must take 30 seconds and the water must be at about 90°C and 9 atmospheres of pressure. The coffee on the right is the only one obtained using these parameters. The extraction time for the one on the left was too short, and for the one in the middle was too long. At first, the volume of the extraction fractions, taken at 5 second intervals (shown above the cups), increases. Then it decreases, with the colour gradually losing intensity.

species. If on the other hand the colour tends towards dark brown with greyish streaks and the "mesh" of the cream is looser and less compact, then the blend is composed mainly of the Robusta species. After sight, the sense of smell comes into play: in order to "sniff" the aromas it is best to stir the coffee, because the layer of cream tends to prevent them from rising. Not only the quantity (or intensity) of the aromas should be judged but also their quality: this is the hardest and most subjective aspect of coffee-tasting, because qualitative judgments on aromas can only be given by "analogy". Thus the aromas of Arabica coffees may be identified as chocolatey, flowery, fruity or "like toast", and the aromas of Robusta coffees may be described as woody, earthy or mouldy. This is an extreme simplification, because the aromas of coffee are made up of about 700 chemical components and the possible combinations are infinite.

Next comes the test of taste and smell (or taste alone if you hold your nose): the characteristics of the taste of coffee are sweet, acid and bitter. A salty taste is not generally to be found in coffee unless it has been damaged by sea water. The sweet taste is mainly perceived by the receptors on the tip of the tongue, the acid taste by those at the sides and the bitter taste by those at the root. This explains why the sweet taste is the first to disappear (the tip of the tongue is more subject to being "washed" by saliva) and why the bitter taste lingers longest. Sweetness and a certain acidity characterise Arabica coffees, whereas Robustas have a pronounced bitterness due to the higher percentage of caffeine (which is bitter).

Lastly the sense of touch enables us to judge the body and astringency of the espresso.

Body, that sensation of "density" that distinguishes espresso from coffees made by any other method, is due to the presence of emulsified oils and colloids and the microscopic bubbles of coffee gas in suspension in the beverage, and is perceived by the tongue and mucous membranes in the mouth. It is probably so highly appreciated because associated with it is a higher content of aromas (the oils are the "vectors" of the aromas) and a low level of bitterness (the colloids "inhibit" the receptors of bitter taste). Astringency on the other hand is a disagreeable tactile sensation, causing the tongue to stick to the mucous membranes. It is caused by certain chemical substances (such as tannins) which make the proteins "precipitate"

The pleasure and appreciation of espresso coffee come from both its flavour and its aroma. *Right:* The taste and/or aroma sensation that can be received from the best samples are symbolically shown *from top to bottom and from left to right.* We have "toasted bread", "flowery", "chocolate", and "fruity". These are the terms in which the taste of different kinds of coffee are generally described.

Notwithstanding the efforts on the part of many designers all over the world to change the basic shape of the coffee cup, very little in this direction has actually been accomplished. Some attempts are shown here. These were exhibited at the "Un café avec..." show held in France in June 1989. *Left:* "Marie servez-chaud" by Aimé Deude. *Above (from top to bottom and from left to right):* "Fantasie pour une anse" by Sylvain Dubuisson, "Hommage à la Reine du Sluamir" by Marco De Guelt, "Tasse et tazzina" by Olivier Gagner, and "Toupie" by Rena Dumas.

from the mucous membranes, chemically bonding with them. Astringency is often found in Robusta coffees and generally in unripe beans of both species.

Now that we have tested and tasted, we are able to give our verdict on the coffee. Of all the sensations that the senses of sight, smell, taste and touch convey to the brain, the one that chiefly determines our final verdict is the sense of smell. Above all because the strength and subtlety of the aromas found in an espresso is hard to equal in other foods or drinks; then because the sense of smell is the one which, in the course of the evolution of the human species, was the first to be perfected in the interests of survival, making it possible to distinguish between good and bad food. The olfactory nerve was so important to our ancestors that it is the only one in direct communication with the brain, without the "filters" represented by the synapses, generally situated among the neurones of the other nerves. Today the sense of smell is no longer necessary for survival, so that many people forget to use it. But, as it is the only sense that puts us in direct communication with the external environment, we can use it to enjoy to the full the pleasures of life; the espresso is one of them, and ready every day to remind us that this is so.

Aside from being a collector's item, this antique coffee pot is also a symbol that harks back to the invention of coffee and its ineluctable bond with human culture and progress. It is also a reminder that, every once in a while, we should stop our mad rushing around in this frenetic world we live in, take a nice comfortable seat, do some tranquil meditating, and — why not? — have a good cup of coffee.

BIBLIOGRAPHY

Jacki Baxter, *Il libro del caffè*, Dilettoso & Co., Milano 1987

Eugen C. Bürgin, *Kaffee*, Sigloch Edition, Künzelsau 1978

R.J. Clarke/R. Macrae, *Coffee – Volume 1: Chemistry*,
Elsevier Applied Science, New York 1985

R.J. Clarke/R. Macrae, *Coffee – Volume 2: Technology*,
Elsevier Applied Science, New York 1987

R.J. Clarke/R. Macrae, *Coffee – Volume 4: Agronomy*,
Elsevier Applied Science, New York 1988

M.N. Clifford/K.C. Willson, *Coffee – Botany, Biochemistry
and Production of Beans and Beverage*, Croom Helm,
Beckenham 1985

Kenneth Davis, *The Coffee Book*, Whittet Books, Weybridge 1980

Kenneth Davis, *Coffee*, 101 Productions, Usa 1987

P.B. Dews, *Caffeine*, Springer-Verlag, New York 1984

Felipe Ferré, *Il caffè*, Silvana Editoriale, Milano 1988

Ulla Heise, *Kaffee und Kaffee Haus*, Olms Presse, Hildesheim 1987

Bernard Rothfos, *Coffee Production*, Gordian-Max Rieck,
Hamburg 1985

Bernard Rothfos, *Coffee Consumption*, Gordian-Max Rieck,
Hamburg 1986

J.W. Rowe, *The World's Coffee*, Her Majesty's Stationery Office,
London 1963

Mariarosa Schiaffino, *Le ore del caffè*, Idealibri, Milano 1983

Michael Sivetz/H. Elliott Foote, *Coffee Processing Technology –
Volume 1*, The Avi Publishing Company, Westport 1963

Michael Sivetz, *Coffee Processing Technology – Volume 2*,
The Avi Publishing Company, Westport 1963

Gene A. Spiller, *The Methylxanthine Beverages and Foods:
Chemistry, Consumption and Health Effects*, Alan R. Liss,
New York 1984

William H. Ukers, *All About Coffee*, The Tea & Coffee Trade Journal
Company, New York 1935

Michel Vanier, *Le livre de l'amateur de café*, Robert Laffont,
Paris 1983

Various Authors, *Caféhäuser*, Nicolaische Verlagsbuchhandlung,
Berlin 1979

René Wilbaux, *Le traitement du café*, FAO, Roma 1961

Gordon Wrigley, *Coffee*, Longman Scientific & Technical,
Harlow 1988